Haiku
Origami
and More

FRIENDSHIP PRESS • NEW YORK

Library of Congress Cataloging-in-Publication Data

Newton, Judith May, 1939-
    Haiku, origami, and more: worship and study resources from Japan/
Judith May Newton and Mayumi Tabuchi.
        p.   cm.
    ISBN 0-377-00217-8: $5.95
    1. Worship programs. 2. Japan—Civilization. 3. Japan—Civilization—
20th century. 4. Protestants—Japan. I. Tabuchi, Mayumi, 1951-   .
II. Title.
BV198.N49   1991
264'.00952—dc20   91-20927
                                                                          CIP

Book design and typesetting by Patricia Kellis
Map by Carol Görgün.

ISBN 0-377-00217-8
Copyright © 1991 by Friendship Press, Inc.
Editorial Offices: 475 Riverside Drive, Room 860, New York, NY 10115
Distribution Offices: P.O. Box 37844, Cincinnati, OH 45222-0844

Manufactured in the United States of America

Contents

Preface   1

Part One: Sampling the Culture   3
    The Japanese Language   4
    Seasons and Holidays   5
    Songs of Seasons   8
    Folk Stories   10
    Poetry by Children   13
    Traditional Toys and Games   15
    Plurality in Japan   18
    Origami   21
    Ikebana   22
    Tea Ceremony   24
    Recipes   25

Part Two: Meeting the People   31

Part Three: Folding in Prayer   55
    Hymns   55
    Prayers   59
    Poems   62
    Meditations   64
    Visual Arts   67
    Dance   73
    Calligraphy   74
    Origami   76
    Ikebana   77
    A Service of Meditation and Praise   79

Part Four: Unfolding a Rainbow   83
    Church and Other Music   83
    Church Life   86

Notes and Permissions   90

日々是好日

Preface

A sturdy red brown bud opens into fragile green. From blossom forms fruit, rounding, darkening, assuming its distinct aroma. A yellow leaf veined with red drifts toward its reflection in the still pool. Stones soften and sink earthward as the snow embraces them.

The seasons unfold and fold in again in the temperate climates of the islands of Japan, stretching more than 2,300 miles in the same latitudes as those from the Caribbean to Nova Scotia. Many traditional arts of Japan's peoples are grounded in sensitivity to the folding and unfolding seasons, the breathing in and out, taking in and letting go on which our human lives depend. Origami literally creates shapes by folding and unfolding paper. Delicate flower arrangements, *ikebana*, and brush painting, *sumi-e*, and short syllabic poetry, *haiku*, represent the harmony and changeableness of nature. Each relies on discipline, learning and concentration to produce a work of art with the naturalness of breath.

In the pages of this brief book you will find samples of these and other arts of Japan, as well as stories, songs, games. You will meet some of the people in Japan, many from the small community of Christians there, hear what inspires them, what concerns them, what they think and talk and sing and pray about.

We have been conscious of folding and unfolding as we have gathered and arranged the words and pictures that form this book.

Folding suggests closing down, preparation for rest or later use. Unfolding hints of growth and stretching, new chances for sharing beauty, faith, ideas.

The author of Hebrews, borrowing from the Psalms, writes:

> In the beginning, Lord, you founded the earth,
>   and the heavens are the work of your hands;
> they will perish, but you remain;
> they will all wear out like clothing;
>   like a cloak you will fold them up,
>   and like clothing they will be changed . . .
> But you and your years will never end.
>   (Hebrews 1:10-12, NRSV;
>   "roll" altered to "fold."

"Folding up" reminds us of our limitations, our clear need to be changed. It points also to God's steadfastness and patient renewal of our tired, raveled ways. "Unfolding" is referred to in Psalm 119:130:

> The unfolding of your words gives light;
> it imparts understanding to the simple. (NRSV)

Here is the promise of unfailing help, the beginning of wisdom that both frees and emboldens.

We invite you to "fold" and "unfold," prepare and do, meditate and witness, learn and share. As you find insights, fold them into your heart and mind. Then let them unfold in a bright embodiment of love and understanding, reflecting God's glory.

*   *   *

Without the assistance of our "reader in Japan," Barbara Mensendiek (UCBWM, Sendai) and our "Mac operators," KADOTA Noriko (associated with Eiko and Kobe Union churches) and Margaret WARREN (UMC, Tokyo), we would have floundered. Sue ALTHOUSE (PCUSA, Nishinomiya) generously lent her critical insights, as did Pastor KITAMURA Soji (Kobe) and Dr. TAKENAKA Masao (Kyoto). Carolyn FRANCIS and Pat PATTERSON, in the midst of preparing the book *Christians in Japan* and the guide *The Way of Faithfulness*, found time to give advice and encouragement, (see the inside back cover). Our gratitude to Audrey MILLER and Carol AMES of Friendship Press for entrusting this project to us. Thanks to our families, and to all the contributors and translators.

Finally, we wish to thank personnel of the Communications Institute, School of Humanities, and Office of International Programs at Kwansei Gakuin University (Nishinomiya) and the Graduate School and Audio Visual Center of Tohoku Gakuin University (main and Izumi campuses, Sendai) for providing services and work space.

*   *   *

Note on names: Ainu, Korean, Japanese and Okinawan names are written family name first. In this book, family names are capitalized in first use. Some church-related abbreviations are explained on page 90.

The sumie (brush paintings) on pages iv, 3, 14, 54 and 82 are by HASHIZUME Tori, a well-known artist. Born in 1921, Ms. Hashizume is a graduate of the Women's School affiliated with Ochanomizu University, Tokyo. She began to study Nihon-ga (Japanese painting) when she was ten, under the guidance of the famous artist NISHIWAKI Tekiho. She herself has been a mentor for others studying Nihon-ga for 25 years now; her pictures have been exhibited in at major museums in Tokyo and also in New York City. She is an associate member of Tokyo Union Church, her home is in Yokohama.

Part One
Sampling the Culture

T he peoples who live on the larger, inhabitable islands of Japan have developed several cultures. This section includes samplings of Japanese traditions: stories, poems, arts, rituals, games, recipes. Brief pieces add notes from the cultures of Okinawa, islands in the south, and of the Ainu people in Hokkaido and islands in the north. Korean people in Japan work to sustain their own language and arts; some of these persons are introduced in later sections.

> "More important than gaining an understanding through reading is gaining an understanding through living. I would hope that the people who read this book would feel like coming to live in Japan."
> KOYAMA Shozo (introduced on page 35)

A Glance at the Japanese Language

Here are some hints on pronunciation of Japanese words. Other languages of Japan include Ainu, Korean, and Okinawan.

Japanese is not a tonal language like Chinese or Vietnamese, although words such as *hashi* change meaning depending on whether the speaker keeps a flat tone for both syllables or raises the intonation on the first or last syllable; these changes make the difference between "edge," "chopsticks," and "bridge"!

Vowels and consonants in standard Japanese are dependable, always pronounced the same way. See the rough approximations below:

a as in "father" (ah)
i as in "marina" (ee)
    (sometimes almost disappears, as in sh(i)ta, "beneath")
u as in "Luke" (oo)
    (also can evaporate, as in s(u)ki, "like")
e as in "get" (eh)
o as in "vote" (oh)

These are short vowels; long ones are marked with a horizontal accent (accents are not marked in this book). Consonants are approximately the same as in English. In pronouncing Japanese, syllables receive almost equal emphasis. Singular and plural take the same form in Japanese; one says, for example, *"kimono* is" and *"kimono* are."

There are three writing systems in Japan: *kanji,* or "Chinese characters" and two *kana,* phonetic systems. The phonetic systems can be learned in a few days; kanji may take a lifetime. Actually, only two thousand Chinese characters need to be learned in Japan (as compared to ten thousand in China). The difficulty is that some characters can be read or pronounced in a dozen different ways.

Here are some examples of kanji: 山 *yama,* "mountain"; 川 *kawa,* "river"; 神 *kami,* "g/God"; 愛 *ai,* "love." The first character can also be read *san,* as in Fujisan, "Mt. Fuji," and the third character as *shin,* as in *shinwa,* "myth."

In the two kana systems, on the other hand, the marks are reliable; they can be read in only one way.

In the *hiragana* system, かわ can be pronounced only as *kawa* (river) and かみ as *kami* (g/God).

In the *katakana* system, used mainly for words borrowed from other languages, コーヒー can be pronounced only as *coh-hee*, "coffee," and イエス・キリスト as *Iesu Kirisuto*, "Jesus Christ."

This chart shows how kanji developed from the shapes of objects in nature.[1]

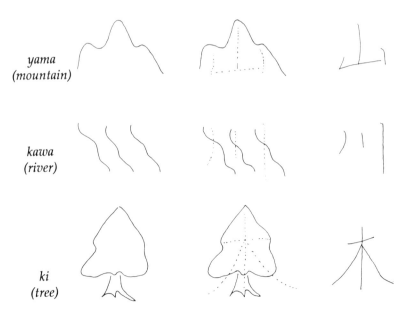

yama
(mountain)

kawa
(river)

ki
(tree)

Once Again Through the Seasons

Surrounded by machines that even out the natural extremes (not too hot, not too cold, not too real) in Japan today, you can still follow the ancient trail of earth's relations with the sun.

Step into the cycle with the aid of the old lunar calendar, when New Year marked the beginning of spring. An ancient poet offered,

> To those who long for spring I would show
> the young grasses pushing up from beneath the snow.

Wait for the plum blossoms that burst on rare branches while it is still cold. Put them with pine and bamboo, "three friends" that symbolize New Year's resolve: to begin again with hardiness, steadfastness, and pliability.

Listen eagerly for the daily weather bulletins to announce, from January in Okinawa to May in Hokkaido, "The cherry front will reach our area by Thursday." Mark your calendar: appointment with cherries at favorite spot. Blossoms cling thickly pink and white on the trees one day; on the next, petal flurries whirl in the wind, speaking to the haiku poet of the transience of life:

"Simply trust: do not also the petals flutter down, just like that?"

And then wait for the first strawberries. Of course, in any month you could have a mass-market greenhouse strawberry. But ah! a natural May strawberry, sweet and perfect in its own time!

Anticipate the start of the Rainy Season about the end of May, and practice not minding the dull soft days, the damp and mold, for you are compensated by neon-bright azaleas, companioned by more greens than you know names for. Hope for late July and the ushering in of the hot humid summer.

Rise early, move while it's cool, give in to mid-day languor, while cicadas bore into you their monotone drone. Here and there, in country or city houses, the icy ring of little brass bells, hung so that a breeze can flutter the poem-card attached to their clapper—a summer wish carried on the sound waves. The sea is comfortable, the cool green mountains beckon. Soon after daybreak, catch the morning-glory fair; at dusk watch for fireflies winking into the night. Look up, search for Vega and Altair, the weaver and the herdboy; can they meet this year too across the Milky Way? Some neighborhood or local town announces a summer festival with "fire flowers." Shooting into the night sky they whine as they rise, pop and crackle in bursting trajectories of color. Be glad for the typhoons that blow summer out to sea.

In autumn evenings, lingering voices of crickets and their relatives tick and tap melodious plaints after sundown. Now the weather bulletins track the advance of autumn color from north to south, setting mountains, hills, and your local temple grounds ablaze in reds and golds. Mark your calendar: appointment with maples at favorite spot. Bring home *nashi* (Japanese pears), *kaki* (Japanese persimmons). Share them with the family, take them to your host. Aren't they a little sweeter this year? Go and gather chestnuts, or ginkgo nuts, to enhance the autumn menu.

The chrysanthemums and camellias cheer you as the year winds through winter's wait, through the Small Cold and the Great Cold. Sip hot tea, your hands also grateful for the warmth of the cup. Eat one more *mikan* (mandarin orange), so easy to peel. Soak in the steamy bath, warm to your bones. Jump into bed and dream of mild weather. And soon the earth will turn around to spring, to begin again.

—Constance E. KIMOS[3]

Holidays

At present Japan has fourteen official national holidays:

New Year's Day (January 1)
Coming of Age Day (January 15)
National Foundation Day (February 11)
Spring Equinox (around March 21)
Greenery Day (the former emperor's birthday; April 29)
Constitution Day (May 3)
A "bridge" holiday (May 4)
Children's Day (May 5)
Respect for the Aged Day (September 15)
Fall Equinox (around September 23)
Physical Fitness Day (October 10)
Culture Day (November 3)
Labor Thanksgiving Day (November 23)
The new emperor's birthday (December 23)

*Minogasa (raincoat/
snowcoat); Kurashiki,
1986*

Photo: Pam Hasegawa

Songs of Seasons

Most people in Japan know these three songs. The original lyrics are included, with new translations into English. "Sakura" and "Haru ga kita" are connected with spring (*haru*), "Kojo no tsuki" with both autumn (*aki*) and spring. *Utaimasho* (Let's sing)!

Kojo no tsuki (Ancient Castle)

DOI Bansui
Trans. by J. M. N.

TAKI Rentaro
Arr. by J. M. N.

1. Ha - ru ko - o ro - o no ha - na no e - n,
2. A - ki ji - n e - i no shi - mo no i - ro,

1. Ban-quet in the cas - tle tow'r, cel - e - brat-ing spring;
2. Morn-ing frost of pal - est hue on the camp in fall;

me - gu - ru sa - ka - zu - ki ka - ge sa - shi - te,
na - ki - yu - ku ka - ri no ka - zu me - se - te,

in the wine-cups go - ing round, moon-light shim - mer-ing;
o - ver-head the wild geese fly, mak - ing mourn - ful call;

chi - yo no ma - tsu - ga - e wa - ke - i - de shi,
u - u - ru tsu - ru - gi ni te - ri - so - i - shi,

seen be - yond the age - old pines moon be - yond com - pare;
lanc - es "plant-ed" tall by tent man - y shin - ing spears;

mu - ka - shi no hi - ka - ri i - ma i - zu ko.
where are glo - ries, where is fame of the by - gone years?

Translation and arrangement © 1990 Judith May Newton.

Sakura (Cherry Trees)

Trans. by J. M. N.

Transcribed by J. M. N.

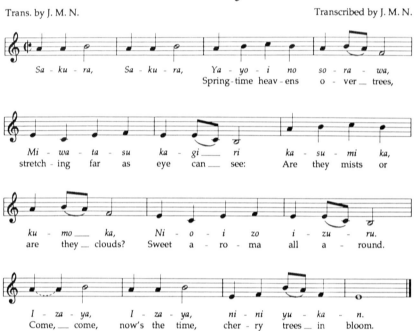

Sa - ku - ra, Sa - ku - ra, Ya - yo - i no so - ra - wa,
Spring - time heav - ens o - ver — trees,

Mi - wa - ta - su ka - gi ___ ri ka - su - mi ka,
stretch - ing far as eye can __ see: Are they mists or

ku - mo __ ka, Ni - o - i zo i - zu - ru.
are they __ clouds? Sweet a - ro - ma all a - round.

I - za - ya, I - za - ya, ni - ni yu - ka - n.
Come, __ come, now's the time, cher - ry trees __ in bloom.

Translation © 1990 by Judith May Newton.

Haru ga kita (Spring Has Come)

TAKANO Tatsuyuki
Trans. by J. M. N.

OKANO Teiichi

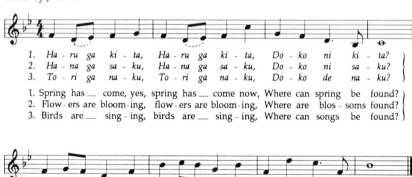

1. Ha - ru ga ki - ta, Ha - ru ga ki - ta, Do - ko ni ki - ta?
2. Ha - na ga sa - ku, Ha - na ga sa - ku, Do - ko ni sa - ku?
3. To - ri ga na - ku, To - ri ga na - ku, Do - ko de na - ku?

1. Spring has __ come, yes, spring has __ come now, Where can spring be found?
2. Flow - ers are bloom - ing, flow - ers are bloom - ing, Where are blos - soms found?
3. Birds are __ sing - ing, birds are __ sing - ing, Where can songs be found?

Ya - ma ni ki - ta, sa - to ni ki - ta, no ni mo ki - ta.
Up in the moun - tains, down in the vil - lage, in the fields and town.

Translation © 1990 by Judith May Newton.

Folk Stories

What can Japan share with North America? To this question a scholar in Tokyo replied, "The simple spirit of the common people expressed in the many Japanese folk stories could be of most help." (KIDA Kenichi, introduced on page 37). The three stories here show the honesty, endurance, and basic kindness of the people. They begin with the New Year (in *fuyu*, winter), go on to cherry-blossom time (around April), and move into summer with Tanabata (a festival in July or August, depending on the region, which marks the end of *natsu*, summer).[3]

The Rabbit in the Moon

Once upon a time, the Old Man of the Moon let his glance fall on one of the earth's forests. There he found a monkey, a fox, and a rabbit, all living together as quite good friends.

"Surely, one of them must be the kindest creature of all," he surmised. "I'll just take myself down there and find out!"

With that, he turned into a poor man and went walking into the forest. "I'm so hungry," he said to the three animals. "Can't you help me?"

Immediately each expressed a desire to help the man and ran off to find something for him to eat. The monkey was able to find some fruit. The fox brought back a large fish. But the rabbit, no matter how hard he tried, could find nothing to offer.

"What am I going to do?" he said. Right away an idea came to him. He spoke to his two friends. "Mr. Monkey, would you mind gathering some wood? And then, Mr. Fox, I'd appreciate it if you'd make a fire with that wood."

Just as the rabbit asked them to do, they found wood and started a fire. It was blazing warmly when the rabbit turned to the poor man and admitted, "I have nothing to give you. But I may be pretty tasty when I'm cooked."

He turned to enter the fire, but was stopped by the words of Old Man of the Moon, for the poor man had changed back to his original form. "How kind you are, Mr. Rabbit. Yet it's not right for you to do injury to yourself. You've proved yourself the kindest, most generous one of all, so I'll see that you have a nice home with me from now on."

With that, the Old Man of the Moon picked up the rabbit. All the way to the moon he carried him. Now, if you look up at the moon on a clear night, you'll be able to see that very rabbit, right where the old man placed him a long, long time ago.

The Old Man Who Made Cherry Trees Blossom

Long ago there lived an old man and woman who always said and did kind things. Right next door lived a couple who were very mean. Now the first couple had a dog, Shiro. They loved him very much and always fed Shiro delicious tidbits. But the people next door threw stones at poor Shiro if he got too close.

One day the kind couple heard Shiro barking away in the farm-yard. The old man went out to find Shiro scratching at the dirt. The man joined in with a spade, which finally clanked against a pot. Inside were many gold coins!

"Thank you, Shiro!" the old man said.

The mean neighbors, who had seen everything, borrowed Shiro and the man roughly commanded, "Dig—or I'll beat you!" All Shiro turned up was some ripe garbage. In anger the cruel man bonked Shiro over the head and killed him.

You can imagine how sad Shiro's owners were. They buried their beloved dog out in the field, planting a little pine there. In a few years it was a full-grown tree. The kind woman said, "I want to do something to remember Shiro by. Let's chop down the pine and make a mortar. Since Shiro loved *mochi* (rice cakes), we can make some in his memory."

That's just what they did. As they started to pound the rice in the mortar, though, suddenly the rice became gold!

Once more the nosy neighbors had been peeping. They borrowed the mortar and pounded away. Again, the rice suddenly changed—but to ill-smelling garbage. Angered, the mean man chopped up the mortar and burned it.

The kind man sorrowfully gathered up the ashes, took them home, and began to scatter them in the garden. Some landed on cherry branches. The cherry trees were bare—it was winter—but immediately they blossomed. Everyone came to see them; even the ruler in his castle heard the news.

As spring came, the ruler was sad because his favorite cherry tree looked dead. Then he remembered stories about the old man who made cherry trees blossom. He had the man brought to the castle garden. The kind old man carefully climbed up the tree and tossed ashes. Sure enough, the tree produced cherry blossoms more beautiful than anyone could remember.

The ruler, who had been watching from horseback, was so happy he called out, "Give this man gold and many presents. And from now on he will be named Hanasakajiji, 'Old Man Who Makes Cherry Trees Bloom.'"

With the ruler's reward, the kind man and woman could live comfortably for many years.

Tanabata Festival

The Tanabata Festival is celebrated in some regions on the eve of July 7, the time when, once a year, Vega, the Weaver Princess star, is supposed to meet her lover, Altair, the Herdsman star, on the bank of the River of Heaven or the Milky Way. According to legend, the celestial princess fell madly in love with the handsome cowherd. The princess was an excellent weaver, and as a reward for her industry and talent the king gave his consent to their marriage. The pair was so much in love, however, that the princess neglected her weaving, and the cowherd allowed all his cows to go astray.

The celestial king became so angered that he finally separated the lovers, forcing them to remain on the opposite sides of the Milky Way. A magpie, seeing the princess' sorrow and feeling great pity for her, assured her that once a year he would build a bridge across the Milky Way so she could be with her lover. Once a year, on the eve of July 7, many magpies spread their wings out, together making a bridge across the Milky Way, and the princess crosses to be with her lover. But, the legend also says, if it rains, the magpies will not make a bridge, and the celestial lovers must wait another year before they can meet.

—Margery L. Mayer[4]

Tanabata Festival, Sendai

Poetry by Children

The Baby Cicada

Insects are a part of everyone's childhood in Japan. Even in the city children can shop for their favorite *kabutomushi* ("helmet beetle") at department stores, with a variety of cages to choose from. In this poem, TANAKA Maki expresses her delight at seeing the emergence and first flight of a cicada. Maki's poem won a prize in an all-Japan contest for school children.

I was at my grandma's catching insects.
A locust flew by.
As I was taking a closer look . . .
  "Oh!"
There was a baby cicada,
    shining in the twilight;
It had pale green wings;
Rocked by the wind,
    it spread them out gently.
It looked like an angel.
I watched it steadily.
It wiggled about.
From atop its "shell" it was catching its breath.
  "Ah!"
It began to take a step.
Slowly, slowly, it began to walk.
Little by little. Slowly, slowly.
I was so glad!
I was so pleased!
"Fly! Hurry, hurry!"

—TANAKA Maki[5]
(Second grade, Fujishirodai Elementary School, Suita, Osaka)

1990 Haiku Contest Winners

Japan has a rich poetic tradition. Haiku (hah-ee-koo) is typically a syllabic poem of three lines, of five, seven, and five syllables. Haiku feature a word that suggests a certain season, following the tradition of it most famous practioner, Basho (1644-1694), who brought his training in Zen Buddhism to bear on the poetic form. These poems are from a poetry contest for students at international schools in Japan, sponsored by the Marist Brothers School, Kobe. The five poems move from spring to winter. Each poem won a special award from a newspaper or local organization.[6]

There's that bird again
Beak deep in frothy blossom,
He doesn't see me.

—Katy LONG, grade 5
Marist Brothers International School, Kobe

Black little spider
Walking on her shiny web as
Sun shines on dew drops.

—MASUMI Hai, grade 5
St. Michael's International School, Kobe

Sound of raindrops
All the windows are closed tight
I'm tired of chess!

—Leina AHUILAR, grade 7
Christian Academy in Japan, Tokyo

Its destiny is
Dawn. The moon marches steady
Silent and resolved.

—Mario AVERBECK, grade 7
Canadian Academy, Kobe

Fresh blankets of snow
Torn by the footsteps of man
Cannot be mended.

—Bethany DILKS, grade 6
Canadian Academy, Kobe

Traditional Toys and Games

What Happened to Daruma?

An Indian Buddhist monk named Bodhidharma has been cele-brated for centuries throughout East Asia as the founder and first patriarch of the Buddhist religious tradition now known in much of the world as Zen. His Indian (Sanskrit) name is Japanized as Bodai Daruma, but the people know him simply as Daruma Daishi or Daruma-san. His large, glaring eyes, heavily bearded jowls, promi-nent nose, and overall severe countenance may confront one almost anywhere. . . Legend has it that the original monk meditated in one position so long, he lost his limbs, eventually becoming a roly-poly, if somewhat dour, toy in souvenir shops.

The staring contest game is played by two children who begin by chanting in unison some version of the following lines:

Daruma-san! Daruma-san!
Let's play the staring game.
If you laugh, you lose!

Immediately, then, each puts on an imitation of the comically serious Daruma and stares intently at the other. The first to laugh is the loser.

In the snow country of Japan, Daruma has yet another place in the play of children. A snowman is appropriately called a *yuki* Daruma (snow Daruma), since the simplest form of a snow figure is very much like the pear-shaped Daruma. [Unlike the three-tiered Western snow person, the one in Japan has only two "rounds."]

During the New Year season, kite-flying events are a time-honored means of celebrating the benefits of the past year and expressing hope for the one forth-coming. Among the most popular subjects appear-ing on New Year kites is Daruma.

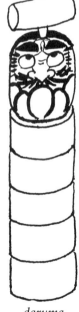

The game called Daruma otoshi consists of five thick rings or disks stacked in an even column and surmounted by a flat-based Daruma figure that has the same diameter as the rings. To begin the game, a player strikes the bottom ring sharply with a mallet in an attempt to knock it clear without upsetting the column. The object is to dispose of each successive ring in this fashion until finally only the upright im-age of Daruma remains.[7]

daruma otoshi

Most children in Japan today know more about baseball or computer games than Daruma otoshi. They may very well fly kites, play tag or collect *kokeshi* for display. But Snoopy and Disney designs are also popular as are modern Japanese cartoon characters.

Wooden or paper daruma are sometimes bought as souvenirs, and a politician often buys a pâpier-maché daruma with Orphan Annie eyes to bring luck to his or her campaign: one eye is filled in at the beginning of the campaign, the other filled in at the end, if the person is elected.

Wooden Dolls and Kokeshi Festival

[One type of *kokeshi*, wooden dolls made in the northeastern part of Japan, is called "Narugo," after a hot-springs town northwest of Sendai.] They have thick, sturdy bodies with squared shoulders, and most have chrysanthemum designs on the bodies, although other flowers or maple leaves are painted on some. Except for small-sized dolls, their heads and bodies come from two pieces of wood, and are fitted together in such a way that the completed dolls make squeaking sounds if the heads are turned slightly. Their eyes are drawn with single crescent lines with small eyeballs underneath (*hitoemabuta*). This, together with small noses and mouths, gives the dolls very gentle but slightly aloof expressions. . . .

naruko kokeshi

In [early August] a kokeshi festival in Narugo, Miyagi prefecture, is observed for three days. On the first day of the festival more than two hundred kokeshi made during the past year by craftsmen all over Tohoku are dedicated one by one to the deity of the Onsen-jinja (Hot Spring Shrine). A year later these kokeshi will be transferred to the Nippon Kokeshi-kan, a small but unique museum of kokeshi, where they are put on permanent display.[8]

—TAKEUCHI Chieko and Roberta STEVENS

Jan-Ken-Pon: A Version of "Rock, Paper, Scissors"

People of all ages play this game based on nonsense syllables. Here are the directions. Both players bring closed fists down partway as they say, "Jan-ken"; then as they say, "pon," each leaves his or her hand as a fist for "rock," or spreads fingers palm up for "paper," or extends first two fingers only for "scissors." If both players put forth the same sign, say "Ai-ko" then "de-sho" (Literally, these words mean, "nobody's a winner"—so let's try again). Then repeat the gestures and the chant until someone wins.

If rock and scissors meet, rock wins because it can smash scissors.
If paper and rock meet, paper wins because it can cover a rock.
If scissors and paper meet, scissors wins because it can cut paper.

This game, played by two people or more, can be used to decide the winner of a tie game (children), the order in which reports are given (students) or even the membership on committees (at faculty or business meetings)!

Proverb Puzzle

For each blank, choose the answer from a. to j. that makes the most sense. Note that 1 and 6, 2 and 3, "teach" similar lessons.[9]

1. *Kobo mo fude no ayamari:* Even Kobo* made mistakes when he used a _____.
    *Kobo Taishi, noted for his skill in calligraphy
2. *Uma no mimi ni nembutsu:* Saying "nembutsu"* into a horse's ear is a _____.
    *a prayer to Amitabha, Buddhist deity
3. *Neko ni koban:* Giving a cat a _____ is useless.
4. *Kurushii toki no kamidanomi:* Only in _____does one rely on God.
5. *Sannin yoreba Monju no chie:* If three people get together, you have the_____of Monju.*
    *Monjushiri, the bodhisattva (enlightened being, regarded as a Buddhist deity) of intellect/thought
6. *Saru mo ki kara ochiru:* Even _____ fall from trees.
7. *Toranu tanuki no kawazanyo:* Figuring your gain when you haven't yet _____ the tanuki* isn't very wise.
    *raccoon dog, formerly sought for its fur
8. *Sendo oku shite fune yama ni noboru:* If there are too many _____ the ship will climb a mountain!
9. *Ishi no ue ni mo sannen:* Even if you just sit on top of a _____, doing it for three years will warm it up a bit, that is, bring some results.
10. *Nana korobi ya oki:* Though you may fall down seven times, you can get up _____ .

    a. captains   f. rock
    b. caught   g. times of distress
    c. eight   h. waste of time
    d. koban (gold coin)   i. wisdom
    e. monkeys   j. writing brush

Answers on page 90.

Plurality in Japan

The Ainu People

You may have learned at school that Japan is at the farthest end of Asia and the Yamato [Japanese] race has been living there from ancient times. I too was told that Japan consists of one race and that everybody speaks one language. But if you open your mind and look around, you will notice that Japan consists of many races. In Japan, there are the Yamato [Japanese] race, Ainu [aboriginal] race, Ryukyu [Okinawan] race, Korean race and others.

According to a book recently published abroad, which tries to classify all the languages in the world, there are six languages in Japan. Unfortunately, the Japanese government, unlike the government of India or Switzerland, acknowledges only one language as an official language.

About two hundred years ago, Okinawa was an independent country, and in Hokkaido the Ainu people lived freely. People could come and go freely. Then the warriors of the south got power and used the Ainu like slaves. After the Meiji Restoration, in 1868, the Ainu became free again, but their fields and mountains were possessed by other people. After many struggles, now young and old are doing their best to protect their culture and reconstruct their own spirit.

—ASAI Toru[10]

Ainu Embroidery, Ainu Songs: Love and Protest

In the old days our men hunted and fished but always with a deep respect for all living things, while our women took pride in their beautiful embroidery, decorating *attushi* (clothes made from the fibers of the inner bark of trees).

Every being with a form has a spirit. The moon and stars, forests and lakes, flowers and trees, birds, everything. With this belief

"The 'Earth' of the Wind"
Chikap Mieko

women worked on their embroidery, transforming beings into living *Kamuis* (spirits) with special powers.

Each movement of the needle, forming a unique geometrical pattern, gives form to spiritual beings. A young girl, thinking about her lover and softly singing a love song, would put her heart into the patterns born from her needlework.

> Beloved one/ I want to see you/
> I want to become a bird,
> so that I can fly to you!

*   *   *

No matter how viciously cornered [in the 17th and 18th centuries], our women never stopped fighting. Their resistance can be seen, for example, in the *ikarakara* (an embroidery design) worked on their clothes. The ikarakara are the eyes of the night-singing *Kamui* (owl), which is a Kamui *chikap* (Kamui bird) and also a Kamui dwelling in the village, guarding it. The Kamui's eyes scowl at evil beings brought in by the [Japanese] colonists, guarding people from the diseases that were "gifts" of these people. The ikarakara, therefore, also embodies the anger of our people. My own ancestors were forcibly relocated in May 1885. Survivors of the forced relocation recall their homeland, by singing an *upopo* (song), which describes their desire to be like the wind blowing through the deep forest, to be like a bird flying high in the sky; this upopo is a *mattu yukara* (women's epic), transmitted by my own great-grandmother.

Although the colonists tried to destroy the culture and tradition of the Ainu by even prohibiting our people from using *Ainu-itak* (the Ainu language), our soul has been kept alive in resistance songs like this [upopo].

—CHIKAP Mieko[11]

Okinawa Fabrics

Bingata, one of the best fabrics, has its popularity because of its beautiful colors, marvelously fine design, and suitability to the climate of Okinawa.

How did the ancient people use bingata?

They used different colors and designs to go with social ranks: for example, yellow color, which expresses the sun, was used for people of the highest rank.

Bingata was mainly used for formal kimono, for screens and curtains. They drew directly on the cloth using a tube stuffed with paste, instead of using a pattern. Although the design was simple, the color coordinates were bold and powerful. They used Bingata

as a wrapping cloth (*furoshiki*), too.* On the cloth people drew cranes and tortoises, symbolizing long life. What is the dyeing process? After they dry the cloth, they begin to paint. For the first painting, they use light colors, for the second, deep colors. This gradation, or "shading," characterizes Bingata.

The young people in Okinawa today love to use bingata, first of all for costumes for Ryukuan traditional dances and also for kimono made of bingata instead of an ordinary Japanese kimono and for neckties.

—YAMAZATO Keiko & members of English Composition
Workshop, Okinawa Christian Junior College[12]

Some Other Arts of Japan

Hundreds of books have been published on the arts and crafts of Japan, many of which were introduced from Korea and China. From pottery to motion pictures, "martial arts" to *butoh* (a recently developed dance form), there is much to discover, admire, and "try to do." Learning by doing can challenge your perspective, open your eyes, and provide exercise for body and spirit.

furoshiki are used for wrapping items to carry, such as books or lunch boxes, or to present, such as gifts traditionally given to guests at a wedding.

Origami: Folding Paper

The charts for this origami and the one on page 76 were prepared especially for this book by Allison Young.

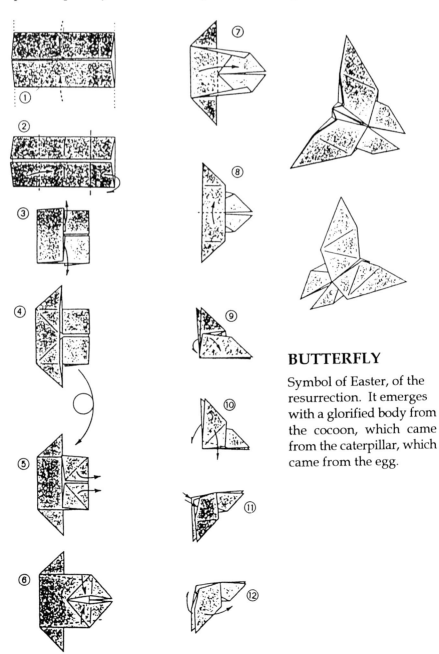

BUTTERFLY

Symbol of Easter, of the resurrection. It emerges with a glorified body from the cocoon, which came from the caterpillar, which came from the egg.

Elements of Tradition

"Japanese who become Christians lose part of their culture. But I find some important elements in Japanese traditional arts, like *ikebana* (flower arrangement) or tea ceremony." —YAMAMOTO Kikuko, co-pastor with her husband of a church in Sendai.[13] In the precise, calming disciplines of Asia one can learn anew to appreciate nature's variety and economy. These are times for the folding and unfolding of one's spirit.

Ikebana (Flower Arrangement)

Most schools of ikebana start new students learning arrangements that express the beauty of form through triangular shapes. The triangle has the beauty of simplicity and is a complete design in itself, having the most basic geometrical shape. The first form taught by the Ichiyo School of Ikebana is called the Upright Form. It uses branches that grow in an upright manner, such as cypress, nandina, pampas grass, pussy willow, plum, cedar, reed, and cattails.

Front View

To arrange the Upright Form, you need an oval or round container that is shallow with straight sides. Place a pin holder (*kenzan* in Japanese: often called a "frog" in English) vertically either to the left or right of the middle of the container. Three main stems cut to different heights and arranged in different directions form the outline of the arrangement. From the material you have chosen, select three that have straight, strong stems: the strongest will be the first main stem, the next strongest the second, and the least strong the third. To determine the length of the first stem, add the diameter of a round container to the height of the container and multiply by 2. The second is 3/4 the length of the first; the third is 3/4 the length of the second.

First Main Stem: Placed upright at the rear of the kenzan.

Second Main Stem: Placed at the midpoint of one side of the kenzan and leaning twenty-five degrees forward.

Left Side View

Third Main Stem: Placed at the front corner of the other side of the kenzan, leaning forty-five degrees forward. [In some ikebana schools, these stems are referred to as *ten* (heaven), *jin* (person), and *chi* (earth).]

Use as many assistant stems as needed to fill in where the main stems seem weak or skimpy.

When the arrangement is nearly completed, there will always be some space or a "vacant spot" in the center. Flowers play the role of filling this space and contributing to the overall stability and solidarity of the design. They also enhance the color effect of the entire arrangement.

The side view diagram of the completed arrangement on the previous page will help you understand the placement of the flowers. Notice that the first (A) flower to be placed has a medium-length stem and the largest blossom, while the second flower (B) has the longest stem and the smallest blossom. The shortest-stemmed flower (C) is placed in last; its blossom medium-sized. When positioned correctly, these three flowers should form a triangle similar to the main stems, except that there is a minimum of space between them.

Left Side View

—Elaine Jo[14]

Arrangement (tall) that fits diagram in Part One

Arrangement by Mr. KASUYA Akihiro of the Ichiyo School of Ikebana.
Photo by OGOSHI Kenichi

Tea Ceremony

The room is utterly simple and quiet. It is the special place in MAEHARA Tazuko's house where she teaches tea ceremony every week. Upon entering, you, the guest, must first admire the hanging scroll and the flower arrangement in the *tokonoma* (alcove). The picture or calligraphy has been carefully chosen to reflect nature and the season. The flowers have been freshly picked from some corner of the garden that morning and arranged simply, in understated fashion.

Kneeling on the *tatami* (straw mat) floor, you swing around to perch on one of the cushions readied in front of the iron kettle, which is bubbling with *oyu* (hot water) over a charcoal fire in a recess in the floor. Your eyes can rest naturally on the small garden outside the window, seen through the rising steam from the kettle.

Meanwhile, the students take turns preparing the tea in a strictly prescribed manner, moving about deliberately, without a word, handkerchief tucked carefully in at the waist. The tea is made by putting *matcha* (powdered green tea) into a *chawan* (a matcha bowl/handleless cup), pouring in hot water, stirring until foamy with a *chasen* (a tea whisk made of bamboo) and then served. As the tea is being made, you are given a sweet, to be eaten first because its sweetness enhances the somewhat bitter taste of the tea.

After bowing in thanks to the server, offering the bowl to the guest on the left, then bowing to the host/hostess, you pick up the bowl with right hand, resting it on the left hand. Then you rotate the bowl twice clockwise, so as not to drink from the front. Holding the bowl in both hands, you drink the tea in three sips, wipe the rim, turn the bowl twice counterclockwise, put it down in front. Having admired the tea cup, you replace it and once more bow in thanks to the server.

When I asked Mrs. Maehara's students, all homemakers, what the tea ceremony meant to them, they answered:

—it quiets my heart, settles me down;
—in the stillness, there is healing;
—through tea, bitter feelings and resentments are soothed, for example, it helps me to be more forgiving with my mother-in-law;
—it's a change of pace in a busy schedule;
—it gives me continuity through all the changes and family moves from one city to another, which I experience because of my husband's job.

I too found it restful, "filling" with its "emptiness," a refreshment of spirit.

Of the various schools of tea ceremony, the kind described above is typical of *urasenke*, based in Kyoto and in 1990 beginning to celebrate the 400th anniversary of the death of its founder, Sen no Rikyu (1522-1591). Behind this ceremony, using a most common leaf, are over four centuries of tradition of tea drinking in Japan, and, through Buddhism, a custom that links all the cultures of East Asia from ancient times.

—Barbara Mensendiek[15]

Recipes

The kind of rice and tea, the way you prepare them, the seasonings you use with various dishes—all these make Japanese cooking and Japanese meals distinctive. Some items that may be better known outside Japan are *sushi* (vinegared rice, packed around cucumbers or pickles, or topped with raw fish) and *sukiyaki* (very thinly sliced beef strips and vegetables, cooked in a shallow broth of soy sauce, rice wine, and sugar).

We offer here some basic helps on preparing rice and tea, a recipe from *Buy It 'n' Try It*[16] for a chicken-and-rice bowl, and two recipes from KOBAYASHI Katsuyo, know to millions in Japan through her books and TV appearances.

Cooking Rice

Be sure to get the short-grain "sticky" rice, if you can. You may have to wash it 2 to 3 times, depending on the brand (check the directions). Then into a heavy covered saucepan put an amount of water equal to the volume of rice, cup for cup, or use 1.2 to 1.5 times the amount of water, depending on your taste, freshness of rice, etc. You can check the amount by placing the tip of your first finger on the surface of the submerged rice and seeing if the water comes up to the first knuckle.

Let the rice stand covered for at least 20 minutes. Turn the flame on high until the water boils. Leave lid on, but lower flame. Simmer for about 20 minutes, until water has been absorbed. Stir with flat wooden spoon, replace lid and let steam on very low heat for 10 minutes or so. Then serve in rice bowls, steaming hot.

Some of the above comes from GOTO Takako, a graduate of Baika Women's College and a cooking instructor in Sapporo. She also has furnished part of the following information on types of tea.

Kinds of Tea; Preparing Sencha

Sencha is the tea most often enjoyed by people in Japan. When people say *ocha* (tea) or *Nihoncha* (Japanese tea), they are referring to sencha. It's a little bitter, so after you drink it, you might like something sweet. *Bancha* is made from leftover, rather tough leaves, so requires very hot water. Parched bancha, with "popped" unpolished rice added, is called *genmaicha*. (Some non-Japanese call it "popcorn tea.") *Mugicha* is made of barley and served hot in winter, cold in summer.

When preparing sencha, warm the teapot first, with a few inches of not too hot water. Also fill the (handleless) tea cups with hot water. Dispose of the hot water remaining in the pot. Pour the somewhat cooled water from the cups into the pot, after measuring a few teaspoonsful of tea into it. Let the tea steep a few minutes. Pour it back into the cups and serve.

Irori *in the Kurashiki Museum of Folkcraft.*

Photo by Pam Hasegawa

Dinner Dishes

Oyako Donburi [Chicken Bowl]

400 grams (almost 1 pound) sliced chicken
4 to 5 round onions, peeled and cut lengthwise
1 bunch of greens—Japanese *mitsuba* (trefoil); if not available, use
   parsley or celery greens
1/2 bamboo sprout, if in season, or canned bamboo sprouts may
   be substituted
1 package *shiitake* [6-7 dried mushrooms], soaked in water about
   ten minutes [or any other mushrooms]
soy sauce—about 1/2 cup to taste
1/4 cup sugar
5 or 6 eggs

Peel and slice onions. Cook in oil in one frying pan while meat is frying in another. When chicken is done, add the onions, other ingredients, and seasonings, and cook, covered, for about 15 or 20 minutes. Beat eggs lightly together and pour over the cooked mixture, replace the lid and cook until the eggs have just set. Serve over rice immediately. Substitute pork or beef for chicken, if you wish.

—Helen Shorrock

Bright and Shining Spinach

[Wash spinach.] Prepare a large pan of boiling water. Put in a pinch of salt—unless you're going to wait a while before [serving] the spinach. Put the leafy end of spinach in first, roots [or stems] up.

Stir the spinach around with chopsticks. Without covering the pan, you'll find the spinach becomes quite soft all over and rather pretty.

Cook according to your own taste, about a minute. To try it, lift out a stalk and test the bottom part with your fingernail.

Turn off the heat and take the spinach out immediately. [Drain it.] Place it in cold water. Take the root [or stem] end in your hand, and swish the spinach in the water, up and down. Dispose of this water and start again with fresh. Repeat this several times.

Finally, place the spinach in very cold, clean water for 3-5 minutes. Taste a bit, and if it's not the tenderness you desire, place it again in cold water for another 2 minutes.

You can eat the spinach with soy sauce or vinegar—or both. If you prepare the spinach this way, you'll really enjoy it. You may think you're losing lots of valuable vitamins and minerals, but that's not so . . . and the taste will prove it!

—Kobayashi Katsuyo[17]

Meeting Kobayashi Katsuyo

When we asked Ms. Kobayashi what Japan can share with North America, she replied: "It would be good if the Japanese way of growing and cooking vegetables could be made known." Elsewhere she has written:

The beauty of flowers can be found by everybody, but how many people notice the beauty of vegetables, since they're connected with ordinary domestic life? The more I cook, the more I discover their beauty. All vegetables are special gifts from God.[18]

To the question, What are your hopes for the 1990s, she wrote, "I hope that experiments with animals (animal vivisection), the making and selling of fur coats and similar apparel, and cruelty to animals will decrease."

When asked about the Scripture passage most meaningful to her, she mentioned Matthew 22:39.

Ms. Kobayashi was born in Osaka and now lives in Tokyo. "I first saw one of her recipes in a women's magazine 15 years ago," remarked KADOTA Noriko:

It was impressive because it was simple, the materials cheap, the cooking a speedy process, but with such good results. I found out she had two small children, and from the time they were very young, she let them play in the kitchen, observing certain rules, of course.

Onigiri (Rice Balls)

In a cookbook for children, Ms. Kobayashi included this recipe. She writes, "This way of making *onigiri* (rice balls) is for children who have difficulty shaping the balls with their hands." Usually you dip your hands into salty water to keep the rice from sticking, and then form balls—or triangles—from the steaming rice (careful! it's hot), pushing a pickled plum or piece of cooked fish into the middle before giving the onigiri its final shape. You may wrap it in toasted seaweed or roll it in toasted sesame seeds.

Cook rice [the "sticky" kind], and prepare *yakinori* [green-black seaweed or laver, toasted], *umeboshi* [pickled plums], baked salmon, etc.

Also, wet a small clean towel and wring it out. Place a cup for green tea [no handles] on the table.

1. Place the towel over the teacup.
2. Shake some salt onto the towel—not too much.
3. Fill the cup about half full of hot rice.

4. Then take the pit out of the plum and put the plum on top of the rice [or use the salmon or other ingredients].
5. Now fill the cup with more rice.
6. Shake some more salt over the rice.

7. Pick the cloth up carefully, putting the four corners together to make a "bag," and hold it tightly.

8. Swing the bag around over your head, being careful not to let go!
9. Finally, holding onto the bag with one hand, take the other and give the bag a turn, squeezing tightly.

10. Open the bag and you will have an onigiri, all made!

11. Roll it in cut-up nori [toasted seaweed], or wrap it in nori, as you please.[19]

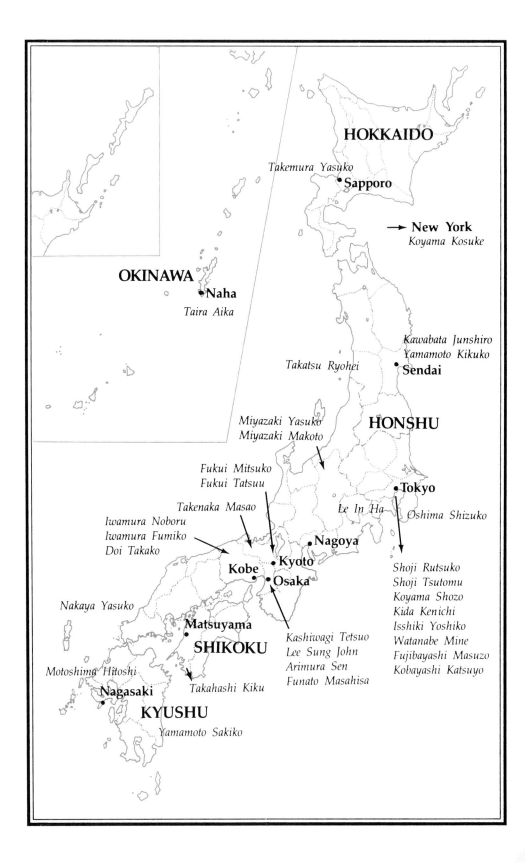

HOKKAIDO

Takemura Yasuko
● Sapporo

→ New York
Koyama Kosuke

OKINAWA
● Naha
Taira Aika

Kawabata Junshiro
Yamamoto Kikuko
● Sendai

Takatsu Ryohei

HONSHU

Miyazaki Yasuko
Miyazaki Makoto

Fukui Mitsuko
Fukui Tatsuu

● Tokyo

Takenaka Masao

Le In Ha   Ōshima Shizuko

Iwamura Noboru
Iwamura Fumiko
Doi Takako

● Nagoya

● Kyoto

Kobe
● Osaka

Shoji Rutsuko
Shoji Tsutomu
Koyama Shozo
Kida Kenichi
Isshiki Yoshiko
Watanabe Mine
Fujibayashi Masuzo
Kobayashi Katsuyo

Nakaya Yasuko

● Matsuyama

SHIKOKU

Kashiwagi Tetsuo
Lee Sung John
Arimura Sen
Funato Masahisa

Motoshima Hitoshi

Takahashi Kiku

● Nagasaki

KYUSHU

Yamamoto Sakiko

Part Two
Meeting the People

*T*he land area of Japan not too mountainous to be inhabited is small compared to many nations with similar-sized populations. And this land stretches more than 2,300 miles from north to south. So to travel to meet people from across Japan would be an extensive— and today an expensive—journey. Yet how can anyone gain a sense of a country and its cultures without getting to know people— where they live, what they do, what they think and believe about themselves, the world and life? Because we could not travel to all parts of the country to interview people, we have used mail and telephone instead. In addition to offering us basic information about themselves, the twenty-two persons whose interviews appear here responded to three questions:

1. **What elements of culture in Japan would you most like to share with people in North America?**
2. **What are your hopes and aims for the 1990s?**
3. **What passage from the Bible do you find most striking?**
   (These numbers are used as a kind of shorthand in many of the interviews.)[1]

We meet these people, many of whom are Christians active in local churches, as if we could begin our journey in the northern island of Hokkaido and then travel south, stopping often for tea and conversation, all the way to Okinawa (with one long side trip to New York). See the map on the facing page.

At the end of this section, we also meet three medical doctors and two prominent Japanese politicians. In addition, because of their special interests and skills, some persons are introduced in other sections of the book.

> "It is my earnest prayer that as Christians in Japan and in North America we will be able to calmly and sincerely communicate with each other across national boundaries in a spirit of love and caring."
>
> (WATANABE Mine, introduced on page 38)

TAKEMURA Yasuko (b. 1933)

Member of National Diet
Sapporo, Hokkaido

1. What elements of culture in Japan would you most like to share with people in North America?

Through its long history Japan has been creating traditions and culture. In the ancient architecture and art work found in Nara and Kyoto there are designs and a sense of color that surprise even those of us in modern times. I think the ideas and polite customs that gave birth to these works are wonderful. However, the attitude of shedding Asia and putting on the West, which resulted from the Pacific War (more properly the 15 years of war dating from the Manchurian Incident in the early 1930s) has brought about great changes in Japanese ideals. Nothing eats away at the human heart like war. However, having lived through this tribulation, we can contribute peace-loving hearts.

2. What are your hopes and aims for the 1990s?

Contrary to all expectations, the Berlin wall has crumbled and Eastern Europe, Mongolia, Tibet and the Soviet Union have begun to move. This movement is entirely one of people seeking democracy.

As a member of the Upper House of the Diet, I am on the Budget Committee, the Foreign Affairs Committee, and the Special Committee on Okinawa and the Northern Territories. I must be sensitive to what is happening in the world. I think Japan is being challenged to decide how it should live in this international society. How can we correct the disparity between the northern and southern hemispheres, or overcome the problems of apartheid, poverty and hunger, or intrusions on human rights?

As a member of the Diet, I want to work seriously for peace in Asia and the Pacific area and to take the lead in the wave of arms reduction. Environmental protection and a nuclear-free society are also my concerns.

3. What passage from the Bible do you find most striking?
Psalm 126:5-6

"It was not surprising to see on the bookshelves of Ms. Takemura's Diet office a biography of Meiji liberation and early antipollution campaigner TANAKA Shozo (1841-1913), a study of Japan's postwar constitution by Socialist Party Chair DOI Takako, and volumes on Hiroshima, feminism, and more."

Ms. Takemura first served one three-year term in the Lower House, was out of office for three years, then won a six-year Upper House term with one of the largest votes in Japanese parliamentary history.[1] She is married and has a son, 27. She is a long-time member of Hokko Church in Sapporo.

KAWABATA Junshiro (b. 1934)
Professor, WCC Central Committee
Sendai

1. Because the confrontation between Japan and the U.S. is based on the question of industrial profits, it is foolish for people of both nations to be involved in such issues. Because "our citizenship is in heaven," don't we need to cross national boundaries and to have more exchanges on a personal level? As long as we don't move beyond nationalism, it will be difficult for any kind of cultural exchange to bear fruit. On this point, it would be best to introduce people in the States to the antiwar movements in Japan during World War II.

2. I would like to participate as much as I can in three areas: the abolition of nuclear weapons, the protection of the natural world—given to us by God—from destruction by human beings, and the solution of the problems of starvation and poverty in the third world.

3. Matthew 25:31-46

Mr. Kawabata, who has served on the Central Committee of the World Council of Churches, is an assistant professor in the Christian Studies department of Tohoku Gakuin University in Sendai, an active layperson in the Kita Church there, translator of Bultmann's *New Testament Theology*, and a skilled organist.

SHOJI Rutsuko (b. 1933)
Educator, NCCJ Staff
Kanagawa Prefecture

1. Zen, flower arranging, and such would be beneficial, I think, for settling into mutual existence with nature and for achieving spiritual liberation. I think they would be helpful in achieving freedom from a competitive society and in recovering human nature.

2. My own policy for this year is to be anti-discrimination and anti-nuclear power. As for movements in the world, attention must be given to protection of nature and solidarity for peace. I think these

relate to the maintenance of respect for life and human rights and to protection of the planet.

3. Philippians 1:9-11

Ms. Shoji, a graduate of Aoyama Gakuin University, is acting director of the Educational Division of the National Christian Council in Japan (NCCJ). She has written on peace and on the rights of children and youth. She is married to Shoji Tsutomu.

Mr. Shoji, a graduate of Waseda and Tokyo Union Theological Seminary, is a seminary professor and chairs the Peace Committee for NCCJ. Among his English works is an article, "Not the Chrysanthemum but the Crown of Thorns: A New Vision of Mission in Japan."[2]

SHOJI Tsutomu (b. 1932)

Professor, NCCJ Peace Committee
Kanagawa Prefecture

1. First, a sense of harmony with nature, a way of daily life that fits with the seasonal changes, and the things that can be seen in religions such as Shinto and Buddhism. With Japan's rapid modernization and technological progress, these values are being lost. However, some people are rediscovering their importance. Then, the spirit of harmony among persons. There is a danger that individual freedom will be suppressed by group consciousness. If, however, we are aware of this danger and work to overcome it, we can move beyond self-centeredness and rejection of "others" and base our society on people living together in mutual support.

2. In the church and community, I want to resist threats to individual freedom in our society, to guard democracy and respect for persons, and particularly to strengthen the movement to protect the human rights of minority persons. Despite the democratization in Eastern Europe, the end of the cold war, and movement toward arms reduction, Japan's armament expenditure has already become third in the world. It is to be feared that Japan's economic power and technological strength will cause further increase in armaments. Working through the NCCJ Peace Committee and joining with citizens' groups in effective activity, I want to correct this foolish, dangerous choice made by the Japanese government and the Self-Defense Forces.

3. Matthew 25:31-46

OSHIMA Shizuko

Social Worker
Chiba

1. Everywhere you can find Japanese who wish to understand the significance of communicating with people in Asia and throughout the world, while realizing the meaning of their "being here." I think it is necessary for these people to speak out to those in other countries, even if their voices are "small" or "unsophisticated." Japanese people really used to like a simple life style, but now are blinded by "convenience." I think it's time for repentance.

2. The individuals in this world, especially in Asia, should live in peace. This is what I would like to have as my goal: as long as I live, I want to work with the people who share this kind of common concern. I do believe that the world—even in its confused state—is moving, little by little, towards the recognition of the tiny voices of the oppressed.

3. Mark 12:31

A native of Shizuoka Prefecture, Ms. Oshima leads an active life in church and community. She not only helped set up the Tokyo Inochi no Denwa (Lifeline), but she also was the first director of the House in Emergency of Love and Peace, a shelter for Asian and other women in Tokyo. With Carolyn Francis she is co-author of *Japan Through the Eyes of Women Migrant Workers* (1988). In the photo also is her husband, Koichi.

KOYAMA Shozo (b. 1930)

Musician, Professor
Tokyo

1. I believe it is vital for us to deepen our cultural exchanges and our understanding of each other's thoughts, customs, and life styles, mutually respecting one another.

2. These days, "trend" has become a popular word. However, instead of going along with this idea of following the latest movement or "wave," I look forward to following a way of living that does not shame, or embarrass, me. I would like to contribute something, even if just a little, toward the realization of a better world for humanity.

3. 1 Corinthians 13

Mr. Koyama, born in Nagano Prefecture, became a Christian after hearing a sermon by KAGAWA Toyohiko (1888-1960). He is a member of Asagaya Church, Tokyo, and a professor at Kunitachi University of Music. Among his compositions is *"Mikotoba o Kudasai"* ("Send Your Word, O Lord").[3]

LEE In Ha (b. 1925)

Pastor, Author
Kawasaki

1. I think we need to call for a rethinking of the mistaken understanding of the Bible which results in a "humanity versus nature" or "humanity controlling nature" formula. Second, I think that while it is not without problems, the family system in which the elderly are cherished can present a meaningful challenge to the North American tradition of radical individualism.

2. In a country like Japan, where the myth of being a single-race culture is still believed, having pride in a differing cultural tradition as resident-Koreans will serve to relativize Japan's single-culture thinking. Upholding our tradition, therefore, has meaning as part of the international trend toward multi-culturalism. The "Kingdom of God," of which the Bible speaks, is expressed as a place in which all of the various cultures of the world have meaning.

3. Luke 4:18-19

Mr. Lee is pastor of the Kawasaki Church (KCCJ) and director of Sakuramoto Kindergarten. He was born in Korea, came to Japan in 1941 and, through the influence of a high school teacher, became a Christian. He studied at Tokyo Union Theological Seminary and in Canada (Toronto, Knox). A past member of the Central Committee of WCC and head of NCCJ and Japan-North America Committee on Cooperative Mission (JNAC), he recently published a series of articles, "A Sojourner's Theology."[4] He is married to LEE Sachiko Sakai, who lost her Japanese nationality when she married Lee, a Korean. She is now naturalized to Korean nationality.

KIDA Kenichi (b. 1930)

Professor
Tokyo

1. What elements of culture in Japan would you most like to share with people in North America?

I wonder if it is possible for the thoughts or customs of one country to be of direct service to the life of another country. However, I think that the simple spirit of the common people expressed in the many Japanese folk stories could be of most help.

2. What are your hopes and aims for the 1990s?

I hope that all people, in every country of the world, will be able to live with their neighbors as equal human beings. Especially, I hope that the 1990 will bring about the protection of the rights of the rapidly increasing number of foreign workers in Japan.

3. What passage in the Bible do you find most striking?

Matthew 5:5

Mr. Kida teaches Old Testament at Rikkyo (St. Paul's) University in Tokyo. Born in Kurashiki, Okayama Prefecture, he has degrees from Aoyama Gakuin, Tokyo Union Theological Seminary, Union Theological Seminary in New York, and Munich. With Lee In Ha, he collected and translated articles on "Minjung" Theology into Japanese.

ISSHIKI Yoshiko (b. 1928)

Writer, Professor, Minister
Tokyo

1. Education in Japan: Children who are trapped in our competitive society and being led into a conformist society are not well developed as individuals. Now they are suffering from many problems, and some refuse to go to school (perhaps as many as 40,000 to 80,000 do so). This situation in our present day society may be similar to that in the U.S. In order to understand our mutual problems, we should dialogue with each other honestly.

Beauty and the Individual in Japan: There are many beautiful aspects of the thoughts and customs of Japan, but if you peel these layers off, you will find some oppressive factors, which prevent the development of the individual, so the beauty may be rather superficial. (The same oppressive factors may be found beneath the surface of close family relationships.)

2. Individual persons can do something for the world. It is important for Japan to have consciousness of the rest of the Asian world, and especially to establish solidarity with women in Asia. Having peaceful relationships with the U.S. in a variety of ways is also very important.

3. 1 John 4:8, 11

Ms. Isshiki, a native of Tokyo, graduated from Gakushuin and Boston Universities and now teaches at Keisen Women's College. An ordained minister, she is on the board of the Japan Bible Society and wants to further "the efforts of feminist theologians in the church in Japan and human rights of Koreans living in Japan, especially concerning the fingerprint refusal movement."

WATANABE Mine (b. 1930)
YWCA Volunteer
Tokyo

1. I have been involved in a number of concrete programs related to justice, peace, human rights, and ecology, as a member of a Kyodan (United Church of Christ in Japan) church and of the YWCA of Japan. Through the YWCA, I've worked in the anti-nuclear movement; for the human rights of Korean residents; with the Conference on Korean A-Bomb Victims; at Sanya Kyodai no Ie preaching point in a depressed area where day laborers live. All of these seem to be different, but it is painful to realize how interrelated they are.

2. I am beginning to see the true meaning of the World Council of Churches' theme, "Justice, Peace, and the Integrity of Creation," in the midst of today's world. With this perspective, I hope this year to continue in these activities, relating to each one with awareness of its importance in daily life. It is my fervent desire that Christians around the world can work and pray together, and that we in Japan can become the salt for change in this secular land.

3. Matthew 25:31ff, Hebrews 13:12-13

Ms. Watanabe grew up in Tokyo as a member of a Buddhist family. Her contacts at Joshi Gakuin and Tokyo Women's Christian College, as well as the words of the Rev. ASANO Junichi—"I think Christianity is worth struggling with"—drew her into that struggle. She has taught at Joshi Gakuin, and from 1982 to 1988 she was national president of the YWCA.

FUKUI Mitsuko (b. 1944)

Social Worker
Shiga Prefecture

1. The other day, I was doing my best to help a girl walk; she can't see and her legs are very weak. I kept pulling and pulling on her arm. Suddenly, she stopped moving. I thought it was strange, but I stood at her side, closed my eyes, and then it hit me. I could hear the sound of a small stream, and the chirping of birds. A breeze brushed past my cheeks. She had heard those sounds and felt the breeze.

Present-day human beings hear the mechanical roar and loud noises around them, but they have a difficult time picking out the quieter sounds like these. Noise is cold. It sets the human heart on edge and makes it feel empty. It represents rationality and civilization. Sound, however, is warm and soft. It provides refreshment. It signifies non-rational emotion and culture. When emotion and culture are lost, joy disappears from human faces, and the human heart is lost.

The treasuring of things which are non-rational and cultural: if persons of North American will also value and protect such things, I feel that peace will come to our world.

2. Human society is filled with pretty words which are self-serving and seek only their own fulfillment. In the midst of that, my life with children who have severe mental disabilities is continually teaching me the following: "'Love is not a pretty word; it is beautiful and warm action."

Our modern world, which is the result of human intelligence and language, has given rise to human arrogance. The arrogance, I believe, is going to lead to the destruction of humanity. In the midst of such a threatened civilization, I pray that my action of living with children will create at least a small amount of bright light.

3. Philippians 4:9

Ms. Fukui was born in Takamatsu (Shikoku), the daughter of a Buddhist priest. She married Fukui Tatsuu in 1964 and now is chair of the Board of Directors for Shiyo Gakuen, a facility for children with severe mental and physical handicaps. She is a member of Notogawa Church (Kyodan).

FUKUI Tatsuu (b. 1932)

Social Worker
Shiga Prefecture

1. For 38 years, I have lived with children who have impaired mental abilities. Recently, the mother of one of those children died. At that time her son said, "Mom's gone to be close to Jesus. I'm not gonna cry." He was laughing happily. He knew I would worry if he cried, so he kept his sadness to himself and laughed for me. When I realized that, my heart felt very warm. Living with these children has very forcefully taught me the following: "If you think and act self-centeredly, you yourself can become prosperous, but that does not create abundance for large numbers of people."

I feel that we have a definite tendency to forget concern for others. Given this, it is very difficult for a society to develop in which all join their hearts and minds in solidarity.

Peace and prosperity will come to this world, not by emphasis on just visible, rational things from a self-centered perspective, but through natural, non-self-centered actions which affirm the value of the hidden aspects of other persons.

2. In our modern-day, profit-oriented society, there is a tendency to value things which are concrete and visible. Thus, in calling and working for the recognition of non-visible, unprofitable things, I often feel weary. However, as a Christian and educator, if I try to avoid those things which are burdensome, I take the joy away from the faces of Christ's children. Therefore, and I stress this, even while thinking, "I'm tired. I'm weary." I keep praying that I can continue, one step at a time, one word at a time, bit by bit, to follow Christ and walk with these children.

Also, I will go on believing that this small activity will be able to halt human society's moving away from God and from the truth.

3. II Corinthians 4:18

 Mr. Fukui was born in Shiga Prefecture and graduated from Doshisha School of Theology. Besides being Director of Shiyo Gakuen, he is on the Board of Trustees of Notogawa Church and serves as president of the Japan Association to Protect Handicapped Children's Right to Learn. Both he and his wife, Mitsuko, have written extensively on faith, hope, and learning from those with handicapping conditions.

TAKENAKA Masao (b. 1925)

Professor
Kyoto

1. Living in a way that responds to the message of nature expressed in the four seasons; involvement in anti-pollution activities similar to that of TANAKA Shozo (1841-1913); and furthering present-day, cultural activities in regional scope, particularly, the type of practical beauty as expressed by the *"mingei* (folk art) movement"—these can be shared with North America.

2. I want to advocate activities that encourage individual abilities and an open and accepting local community, for example, the work of the Nishijin Community Center in Kyoto.

3. II Corinthians 4:7-18

 Born in Beijing, China, Mr. Takenaka studied at Kyoto University, Doshisha and Yale. He is a professor at Doshisha School of Theology, and chairs the Asian Christian Art Association. Of his many publications, some English works are *Christian Art in Asia* (1975, 1983), *God Is Rice* (1985), *Biblical Prints of Sadao Watanabe* (1987), *That All May Be One* (1987), and *Consider the Flowers* (1990), a study of ikebana arranged to express biblical themes.

KASHIWAGI Tetsuo (b. 1939)

Medical Doctor
Osaka

1. Here are some ways in which Japan can contribute to societies in North America:
  — to have more "home stay" programs between countries, and not just ones sponsored by companies;
  — to value and encourage close bonds among family members;
  — to incorporate the beauty of nature in everyday life.

2. I hope every person in the world will accept his or her death as a reality, will carry on with living, while facing the prospect of dying.

3. Revelation 3:8

Mr. Kashiwagi is a graduate of Osaka University and a member of the Mennonite Brethren Church in Ishibashi. He is vice superinten-

dent of Yodogawa Christian Hospital, Osaka, as well as director of the hospice there. When Jean Joyce died in the hospice in 1990, says her husband, Jim, Dr. Kashiwagi came immediately and led in prayer, naturally, comfortingly, faithfully— just as he had been providing medical and spiritual care all along.[5]

LEE Sung John (b. 1952)

High School Teacher
Osaka

1. What elements of culture in Japan would you most like to share with people in North America?

Japan values first of all the good of the group, and then that of the individual. It is said that Japan is a democracy, but that is not completely true. Generosity is shown to people of the same group, but these people find it hard to accept those from outside the group. This makes it difficult to solve problems of racial discrimination and of discrimination against minorities here.

The idea of human rights has not yet been established. Among Japanese customs there are only a few things that can be "contributed" to the people of North America.

2. What are your hopes and aims for the 1990s?

This is the time to think about how to solve racial or ethnic problems and how to spread democratic ideas. Promoting understanding between North and South Koreans and Japanese will further Japan's internalization, will do away with the exclusive social system in this country, and will lead to world peace and stability.

3. What passage from the Bible do you find most striking?

Galatians 5:1-6

Mr. Lee, a graduate of the International Christian University, is among the very few Korean residents in Japan to be hired by a Japanese high school. He is now chairperson of the English Department at Baika High School, Toyonaka, Osaka Prefecture. (He is the son of Lee In Ha; see page 36.) In the photo are Lee Sung John, his wife and their two sons, on left, and his sister and her family on right.

ARIMURA Sen (b. 1951)

Social Worker/Cartoonist
Osaka

1. I am one person who feels the pain of the current economic and cultural friction between Japan and various foreign countries. Not all Japanese are strange workaholics, crazily investing in real estate and stocks, racial exclusivists, or people revering the emperor. There are many individuals and organizations in Japan that are saying a firm "No" to the negative aspects of present-day Japan.

I myself am squirming, suffering, and struggling in daily life. I express this in cartoons. I think the ideas, activities, and publications of such anti-establishment groups should be publicized more and more in North America. It is my belief that when the people of North America get an image of the other side of Japan, a side that is searching for and aiming at making democracy a reality, their view of Japan will change. Then surely we can encourage each other, help each other, as we go on toward a common goal.

2. I draw cartoons to express the misery of people living in Kamagasaki (Osaka), which symbolizes the hidden side (and lowest level) of capitalism, and thus I pose questions to society. As a result I am indicting the shady side of capitalism (the dehumanizing effect of efficiency-first, the mammoth inequality in society, the

Do you know the meaning of "nouveau riche"? It means people who are suddenly rich, through investment!

And the "New Poor". . . they're the people who go bankrupt. . .

So, what does that make us?

It's obvious!

We are the "Traditional Poor"

If you say it in English, that makes us sound really fashionable, doesn't it?

increasing number of homeless persons, miserable working conditions, and the deterioration of family life).

However, I think that the '90s will be an era that will see a joining together in one great tide for the common goal of thoroughgoing democratization and the realization of equality, both on a domestic and a global scale. I believe that my work will naturally blend into this great tide.

3. I am a sort of atheist, so I am sorry and a bit embarrassed to say that I know almost nothing about the Bible. However, I have great respect and appreciation for the Christians who work with dedication for the weak in society, such as the day laborers in Kamagasaki and the homeless. I have many such friends and acquaintances.

Mr. Arimura graduated from Ritsumeikan University, Osaka, in 1975. Since then he has been working at Nishinari Workers Center, drawing cartoons for the Center bulletin for the past 13 years. Among his cartoon creations are three books about "Kamayan," a day laborer in Kamagasaki; Volume 3, *The Alternative Side of the Rising Sun* (1989), has English captions and comments.[6]

TAKAHASHI Kiku (b. 1911)

Social Worker
Matsuyama (Shikoku)

1. The Japanese people fundamentally appreciate clean, pure things; beautiful things; prospering things; eternal things.

My elder sister died as a military nurse in the Russo-Japanese War (1904-5). Her legacy to me was her Bible. On the front cover of her Bible this is written: "No one has greater love than this, to lay down one's life for one's friends" (John 15:13). When I was fourteen, I was captured by her way of living and by this great love of God. Because of these words that my sister left for me, I became an evangelist (*dendoshi*) and have worked as God's servant.

The Greater East Asia War (World War II) took place at this time, and twice my home was bombed. My life was saved, but each time I lost all my possessions. At that time, I received these words of Christ, "Feed my lambs" (John 21:15-17). From that time until now, for forty-five years, I have been working in a lively, fresh way for the Triune God.

2. After being in the midst of destruction, we have been blessed and given life, under the Spirit of Christ, right up to this present moment. By this living faith we gain oneness of belief. I do believe it is a most blessed thing that all brothers and sisters of the world are being brought together as one in Christ.

I have been happy to meet many sisters and brothers overseas through this belief in the Lord: "Very truly, I tell you, anyone who hears my word and believes him who sent me has eternal life. . ." (John 5:24). I earnestly pray that all may be brought alive in this faith, a belief in this "oneness in the Lord," regardless of race, boundary, or denomination.

3. Matthew 24:35, 6:33

Ms. Takahashi named a home for children, which she founded and directed, *Shinboai no Ie*, or "House of Faith, Hope and Love." It is located in Matsuyama, northern Shikoku. She was born in Fukuoka Prefecture (northern Kyushu) and graduated from Lambeth Women's College (now Seiwa University, Nishinomiya). She is currently a trustee of Koinonia Church in Matsuyama.

NAKAYA Yasuko (b. 1934)
Homemaker/Cafeteria Worker
Yamaguchi

2. I'm really concerned about my husband's soul being worshipped at Yasukuni Shrine. The only way that I can really be free is when his soul is "freed." I've come to understand, through the sixteen years of court procedures, that the matter of removing my husband's soul from enshrinement is a very difficult matter.

From now on, in my daily life, I'd like to keep close watch on the ways of thinking connected with Yasukuni Shrine.

Recently I formed a group called, "Protesting Enshrinement: Seeking Minority Rights." We want to link up with other groups that are promoting peace and human rights, and carry on small-scale activities. During the next decade we hope to go forward year by year.

3. Philippians 1:29

Ms. Nakaya was born in Yamaguchi Prefecture, at the southwest end of Honshu, Japan. She lives there now, has one son, attends Shin'ai Church, and is employed as a food server in a school cafeteria. Her husband, a member of the Self-Defense Forces, died January 12, 1968, in a traffic accident. In May 1972 she received notification that her husband's soul had been enshrined (placed in a national Shinto shrine for war heroes), against her will. With the encouragement of her friends, she took the case to court. Lower courts all supported her case, but the Supreme Court turned down her suit, 14-1. ITO Masami, who wrote the minority opinion, cited an earlier minority ruling by the Supreme Court judge, **FUJIBAYASHI Masuzo.**

In his response to the three questions, **Mr. Fujibayashi** (b. 1907) suggested the Japanese samurai spirit might be shared with North America and recommended the English work, *Bushido, the Soul of Japan* (1899) by NITOBE Inazo. Now retired and living in Tokyo, he expressed these hopes for the future: respect for basic human rights; protection of freedom and peace. He finds Job 1:21 and I Corinthians 10:13 to be especially inspiring.

YAMAMOTO Sakiko (b. 1931)
Pastor
Miyazaki Prefecture, Kyushu

1. I am not especially interested in North America. I would rather think about Asia or Palestine instead. Last year I visited the Philippines. There one can discover the strong political power of the United States in that country. I wonder how the Christians in the U.S. feel about the policy of their government.

2. As for the above, I hope that American Christians will try to mold public opinion and take leadership roles in their society. As for my own local situation, the members of my small church are growing older. In the past three years, ten young people have left the church and this community to find work in the city. I feel very sad. I wonder about the future of the churches in rural areas. My goal is to nurture the next generation.

3. Mark 8:34

Ms. Yamamoto graduated from Doshisha University, Kyoto. She is now serving the Hyuga Shinsei Church, on the southern island of Kyushu. In May 1989 she was elected to the position of associate moderator (district superintendent) of the Kyushu District. No other woman in the Kyodan has been chosen for this office in the church.

TAIRA Aika (b. 1968)

Student
Okinawa

1. Even if you say, "Japan-U.S. relations," Japan and Okinawa have different histories and different cultures, so I'd rather think about "Okinawa-U.S. relations."

As in the States you have a history of Native Americans, we too have a history of native people, the Okinawans (Uchinanchu). In order for us to understand each other, it is important to know this fact. We can find out what kind of country Japan is by studying how Japan has dealt with people in Okinawa, just as we can discover the United States or Canada's character by analyzing how those countries have treated native peoples.

However, Japan has suppressed the bad parts of its history, so the real history of Japan does not appear in school textbooks. So it's difficult to discover all this. How about America?

2. The Japan that can't seem to keep from destroying nature. . . The Japan that cannot seem to stop heading toward war again. . . I would like to be the one who can stop this destructive movement. First, I have to make many friends who think the same way. (It's nothing much, but, for example, to keep from harming the environment, I always take along my own chopsticks, and do not use disposable wooden chopsticks, *waribashi*.)

3. II Corinthians 12:9-10

Mr. Taira was born in 1968 in Okinawa, not far from a U.S. Air Force base from which bombers were taking off for Vietnam. "I was born in the midst of those painful days. In the Bible, the book of Lamentations is called *Aika*, songs of suffering. My name takes on the same pronunciation, but with different *kanji*, meaning 'love fragrance.' After high school I spent about three years in a kind of 'free' existence. This year I'm attending Takasaki Junior College of the Arts, studying music education."

KOYAMA Kosuke (b. 1929)
Professor, Missionary
New York City

1. Unless we have a dialogue in which we've invested time, energy, and compassion, we cannot make any contribution. From this dialogue we can renew our thoughts about Japanese ideas and customs. Out of this something very new may emerge. Almost all the ideas in Japan are "imputed." So we must think about this, as well. From the idea of "hospitality," perhaps some kind of meaningful dialogue can develop and lead to some sort of contribution.

2. I think we should lead our lives as if the whole earth were Noah's ark. I would like to work for that kind of theology.

3. Hosea 6:6

Now professor of Ecumenics and World Christianity at Union Theological Seminary in New York, Mr. Koyama and his wife, the Rev. Lois Koyama, as Kyodan missionaries have also served in Thailand and New Zealand. Among his books on theology are *Waterbuffalo Theology* (1974), *Three-Mile-An-Hour God* (1979), and *Mt. Fuji and Mt. Sinai* (1984).

Three Doctors from Japan

I remember that during the early days of my life in seminary, when I became acquainted with the Japan Overseas Christian Medical Cooperative Service (JOCS), a non-governmental organization founded in 1960. JOCS sends medical doctors, nurses, public health care workers, and nutritionists to other countries, while inviting people from overseas to come for training in health care education.

In the Osaka JOCS office, I did volunteer work once or twice a week, meeting Christian people of my own age. One of them was an enthusiastic young medical student, FUNATO Masahisa.

When Masahisa was a fifth-year student at Nara Prefectural Medical College, he visited the Iwamuras, who worked with JOCS in Nepal. Later he described Dr. Iwamura as a great man, energetically working in Tansen and Kathmandu: "The main purpose of this trip was to learn from the people and their faith. I truly encountered God's searching love there. I also went to absorb the energy of Dr. Iwamura!"[7]

Today Dr. Funato is head of pediatrics at Yodogawa Christian Hospital, Osaka, founded by the Presbyterian Church in the U.S., in 1956. My daughter was born in this hospital nearly eleven years ago. Masahisa arranged for my husband to be with me when I delivered her. I was able to listen to doctors, nurses, and my husband, all encouraging me. That was a wonderful experience for my family.

It seems to me that my friend is living out the faith, love, and energy of that early experience in Nepal.

*　*　*

Next come an extraordinary couple, Dr. IWAMURA Noboru, a medical doctor, and Mrs. IWAMURA Fumiko, a social welfare case worker. I always put their names side by side because they worked abroad together from 1962 to 1980 under JOCS sponsorship. They were also both helping in Thailand in 1988. Besides, even in public, Dr. Iwamura does not hide his affection for and appreciation of his wife.

How did Iwamura Noboru become interested in medicine? When he was a high school student in Hiroshima, he was seriously injured by the atomic bomb blast on August 6, 1945. After two days, young Noboru was rescued by some sailors. When he received a letter from one of those kind sailors, suffering from radiation sickness, he felt a call from God to be a doctor. Many years later Noboru carried this precious letter with him all the way to Nepal.

Though the couple have no offspring, they have brought up twelve Nepalese children. Their home in Nepal was filled with laughter and prayer. They shared themselves with the people of Nepal and were ready to learn from them. They taught Bible to the children and welcomed visitors from many parts of the world with warm hospitality.

The Iwamuras

The Iwamuras returned to Japan, Noboru teaching for a time at Kobe University and helping to set up Peace, Health, and Human Development.

I'm sure that the Iwamuras themselves have no idea of the number of lives they have touched and influenced with their acts of caring and healing.

Another couple who worked abroad in mission are MIYAZAKI Yasuko and her husband, MIYAZAKI Makoto, both medical doctors. Between 1963 and 1988 they worked in Bangladesh and Nigeria. Only once did I meet Miyazaki Yasuko, at a church in Kobe, where she gave an excellent presentation of the couple's life and work.

Dr. Miyazaki Yasuko is a pediatrician, but in Bangladesh she also assisted with childbirths and did surgery. The Islamic and Hindu women valued her presence immensely, because they definitely wanted a medical professional of the same sex to give them a checkup. In 1983 she had to do plastic surgery when her husband was seriously injured in a car accident in Bogra.

When I asked Dr. Miyazaki what verses of the Bible spoke to her most concretely, she immediately cited Revelation 3:20. She added that she would like to be a Christian whose heart is open to the love of God, as in this passage. For she knows that she has been supported by countless people, who opened their hearts and prayed constantly for her and her work.

Surely her writings about the validity of different cultures and her reasoned, persuasive speeches will have an impact on the rather closed nature of Japanese groups, in and out of the church. Christ is surely knocking at the door of hearts here in Japan.

Three doctors—Funato, Iwamura, Miyazaki—using their expertise to assist others in the name of Jesus Christ; listening to and living with people of many backgrounds and faiths. Thank God for such witnesses!

—Tabuchi Mayumi

MOTOSHIMA Hitoshi

Mayor
Nagasaki

From a Japanese newspaper:

SHOT BY RIGHTIST: NAGASAKI MAYOR MOTOSHIMA —A MAN WITH STRONG BELIEFS—

The mayor of Nagasaki, Motoshima Hitoshi (67) was born in a small village on the Goto Islands, Nagasaki Prefecture. Historically, this village is known as a *"Kakure Kiristan* (Hidden Christian) village," where Japanese Christians secretly kept faith alive during the Bakufu Government's persecution of Christianity (early seventeenth to mid-nineteenth century). All residents of the thirty homes are Roman Catholics.

Motoshima himself is a devout Catholic. He is a man who has worked hard and accomplished much. Despite severe criticism and threats in reponse to his statement a year ago that "the Showa Emperor (Hirohito) shares responsibility for the war," he has not backed down or changed his stance.

On January 18, 1990, Mayor Motoshima was shot in the back. Those around him were heard saying, "What we have feared has finally happened."

What statements has Mayor Motoshima made in the past, and what kind of man is he, who does not bend his faith at any cost?

"Based on my reading of foreign books, Japanese history, and from my own experiences in the military, I believe the Emperor shares responsibility for the war." (December 7, 1988, Nagasaki City Council meeting, in answer to a question by Assemblyman Shibata of the Communist Party.)

"I respect the Emperor, as the symbol of our country, but I still believe he shares responsibility for the war. If the Emperor had decided more quickly, the war would have ended earlier. Many people died in the atomic bomb blasts, and even 43 years later, people continue to die." (December 12, a press conference)

"I pray for the repose of the Emperor's soul from the bottom of my heart. At the same time I pray for the spirits of all the victims of the war." (February 24, 1989)

Mayor Motoshima worked while going to school and in 1944 was drafted into the Navy. At the end of the war, he returned to Sasebo. The next years saw him both teaching and becoming increasingly involved in politics. In 1979, he was elected as mayor of Nagasaki.

Said an employee of the town hall in his hometown, "We know what hardships Motoshima has been through in becoming mayor. He is the pride of our town. He has deep faith, and is not the kind of person you can dislike. I cannot believe what happened!"[8]

On August 9, 1990, newspapers carried stories of Motoshima's speech on the anniversary of the destruction of Nagasaki. For the first time, a mayor of one of the A-bombed cities urged that Korean *hibakusha* (atomic bomb survivors), who had been forced to come to Japan as laborers, should be given preference in receiving treatment and financial support.

On December 15, 1990, it was announced that "The Nagasaki District Court sentenced Saturday a 41-year-old ultra-rightist to twelve years in prison with hard labor for attempting to kill Nagasaki Mayor Hitoshi Motoshima last January. . . In the ruling, the judge called the shooting an attempted murder and a 'violent and malicious act aimed at eliminating the opinion of a statesman with a different view.' He added: 'This can damage the very foundation of a democratic society. No violence against freedom of speech can be condoned.'"

From 7300 *Letters to the Mayor of Nagasaki*:

"Happy New Year! I think you are great, because you said the emperor shares responsibility for the war." (YAMASHITA Seiko, 12 years old)

"The failure to seek justice and childish timidity in facing facts are common attitudes in our society." (NAKAO Nobuo, 39)

"I saw many Japanese soldiers kill fellow citizens in Okinawa for fear of the American invading force. They were part of the army of the Japanese emperor." (ENOGAWA Anpo, 55)

"I have had the same opinion as you since the beginning of the war, but I could not speak out. So I was overjoyed when you spoke out. I support your opinion with all my heart." (TOYOSHIMA Chieko, 75)

"Hello, Mayor, I am in grade six. I studied about freedom of speech in school. But my parents said we can not enjoy it in our society. You practice now what my textbook says. I want to be like you." (HASHIMOTO Nozomu, 12)[9]

DOI Takako

Member of National Diet
Chair of Social Democratic Party of Japan

Doi Takako is a congresswoman. Born in Kobe, Hyogo Prefecture, on November 30, 1928, she received her bachelor's degree from Doshisha University, Kyoto, in 1951, her master of law degree in 1956. She was a lecturer at Doshisha, Kwansei Gakuin University, and Seiwa Women's College before being elected to the Lower House in 1969. She served as vice chairperson of the Socialist Party during the years 1983-1986 and presently heads that party, elected to the post in 1986 and twice re-elected.

She rendered remarkable services in the amending of the Japanese Nationality Act (1984), which had been unfavorable to women. She is well-known as the first chairwoman of a political party in

Japan. As a scholar of the law, she is devotedly making efforts to ensure that the government observes and maintains the Japanese Constitution.

She always stands by those who have "weaker" positions in society. She responds to them herself, even when they call her early in the morning or late at night. As a representative of women, she helped increase the number of congresswomen in the last election (1989). Her existence itself is encouraging all the women in Japan who have been treated in restrictive ways.

—YAMAMOTO Keiko, Nishinomiya

YWCA Members Visit Ms. Doi

When leaders from the YWCAs of Japan and the USA met Ms. Doi in November 1989, she told them that the interests of Japanese women are changing. They are concerned about many issues beyond their own family life. Ms. Doi (a member of Kobe YWCA) feels the time has come for women to take a more active role in public affairs. For women to be instrumental in changing our society, men's ways of thinking and viewing must be changed. However, it is essential, of course, for women themselves to change, too. Ms. Doi's hope is to have 2,000 women serving in both local and national Assemblies by the year 2000. She felt it was possible if all women's organizations working toward a common purpose would come together.

—Hatsumi MOSS[10]

Back row, from left: Sharon Bettinelli (YWCA, USA), DOI Takako, Hatsumi MOSS and EJIRA Mihoko (National vice pres. and pres., YWCA Japan). *Front row:* Margaret WARREN (YWCA Japan staff), Barbara POWELL and Betty FONG (YWCA, USA).

Part Three
Folding in Prayer

Here we glimpse ways to express, through various arts, faith that is firmly Christian. The forms of all these expressions arise from the cultures of Japan. These forms include hymns, prayers, poems, meditations, painting, sculpture, printmaking, dance and ikebana. In such a rich setting, "folding in prayer" evokes not only the traditional Christian posture of worship but the joys and concerns that faith enfolds: justice, thanksgiving, beauty, commitment, peace, with respect and care for God's whole creation.

> "It is important to understand and express the Biblical message through Japanese culture."
>
> Takenaka Masao (introduced on page 41)

Hymns: Enfolding Old and New

A Pilgrim Song

Most hymns sung in Japan have tunes in the Western modality. The words of a large proportion of these have been translated from English and other European languages. A smaller group of hymns are original Japanese poems set to Western tunes. "Alone on the Mountain Path" is a classic example of this type.

The hymn writer, NISHIMURA Sugao, was born in Matsuyama in 1871 and became a Christian as a young man. After studying for a while in Kyoto at Doshisha University, he returned to Matsuyama, where he met Miss Cornelia Judson, a Congregational missionary, and together they started Matsuyama Yagakko, an evening high school for working youth. Nishimura became the principal of the school, which he served with distinction for sixty-two years.

In February 1903 Nishimura had made the arduous trek to Uwajima to help with some evangelistic meetings. The railroad had not yet been built, and the trail led over steep mountains. On the return trip, Nishimura started out at 10 a.m., walking in the straw sandals of the pilgrim. He reached Tosaka Pass about sunset, with some ten miles yet to go to reach his stopping-place at Ozu.

He decided to compose a poem to his favorite hymn tune, "Golden Hill." The hymn describes the beauty of the mountains as well as the loneliness Nishimura felt. As he walked along by starlight singing successive verses, his heart gradually became lighter, until he felt very happy by the time he reached Ozu at 10 p.m.

A new hymnal was being published that year, and a friend on the hymnal committee submitted Nishimura's hymn. Perhaps partly because the tune is close to Japanese modality, this hymn quickly became one of the most popular in the book. It has had a part in leading many to the Christian faith and has been a touchstone to many others as they coped with the steep places in life's journey.[1]

—Sue Althouse

Alone on the Mountain Path

Sugao Nishimura, 1903
Trans. by Sue Althouse (vs. 1-2, 4-5)
and Judith May Newton (vs. 3), 1990

Golden Hill

Aaron Chapin, 1805

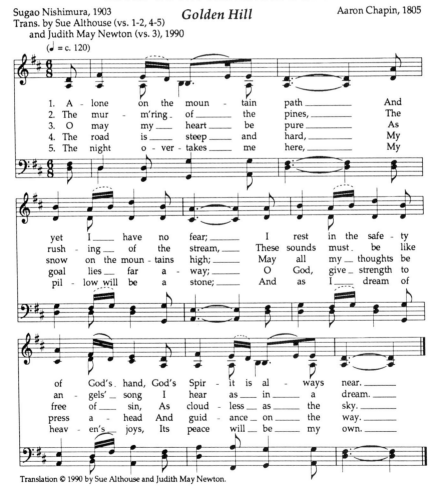

(♩ = c. 120)

1. A - lone on the moun - tain path ____ And yet I ____ have no fear; ____ I rest in the safe - ty of God's hand, God's Spir - it is al - ways near. ____
2. The mur - m'ring _ of ____ the pines, ____ The rush - ing _ of the stream, ____ These sounds must _ be like an - gels' _ song I hear as ____ in ____ a dream. ____
3. O may my ____ heart ____ be pure ____ As snow on the moun - tains high; ____ May all my _ thoughts be free of ____ sin, As cloud - less _ as ____ the sky. ____
4. The road is ____ steep ____ and hard, ____ My goal lies ____ far a - way; ____ O God, give _ strength to press a - head And guid - ance _ on ____ the way. ____
5. The night o - ver - takes ____ me here, ____ My pil - low will be a stone; ____ And as I ____ dream of heav - en's ____ joys, Its peace will _ be ____ my own. ____

Translation © 1990 by Sue Althouse and Judith May Newton.

On Translating Hymns

Existing Japanese hymnals have relied largely on translation. One of the knottiest problems is the great difference in the number of syllables needed. A simple mathematical count of all of the syllables of "Jesus Loves Me" translated into Japanese reveals that only 55 percent of the content of the original has been captured in Japanese. Professor HARA Megumi illustrates this problem with hymns from the early Meiji period to the present day. His first example is *"Shu ware o aisu,"* "Jesus Loves Me." Unavoidably, key concepts are omitted.

Shu ware o aisu, Shu wa tsuyo kereba,
Ware yowaku tomo, osore wa araji.
Waga Shu Iesu, waga Shu Iesu,
Waga Shu Iesu, ware o aisu.

If we were to translate "Jesus Loves Me" back into English, the meaning would be: "The Lord loves me; Since the Lord is strong, even though I'm weak, I won't be afraid. My Lord Jesus. . . loves me." [2]

Using Traditional Music

Finding inspiration in the Bible and their own faith experiences, some writers have matched words of witness with familiar folk or classical melodies. Kyodan and other hymnals include a few examples. "In Your Grace" is sung to *Kojo no tsuki* (music on page 8; also see page 81).

In Your Grace

1. Bite of early morning breeze, Clover next to pine,
   Bright persimmons after rain—Autumn's bold design.
   Thankful for the bright array, Colors, textures, forms,
   We can see the Maker's art, In both calm and storms.

2. Chanting, jogging, barefoot now, Through the snowy air,
   Holding lanterns, ringing bells, Folk climb shrine way stair.
   Burning of the New Year straw, Coming of the Kings;
   We can honor God for all Gifts that winter brings.

3. Pale against the cobalt sky, Cherry blossoms ride,
   Covering the slopes and parks, Lilt on riverside—
   Gone like wisps of smoke in spring, So the green leaves grow;
   Jesus fell to rise again, Lives so "blessings flow."

4. Dragonflies along the wire, Crows awake at dawn,
   Insects rasping in the bush, Picnics on the lawn.
   In the rhythmn of our days, May the Spirit bring
   Time to listen gratefully, Time to rest and sing.

—Judy Newton[3]

Sheep Fast Asleep

Hitsuji wa nemureri
Genzō Miwa, 1907
Trans. by John Moss, 1957, alt.

KŌRIN 4443. 87. 4443. 86
Chūgorō Torii, 1941

1. Sheep fast a-sleep, there on a hill; Grass for their bed, all is still.
2. Star in the sky, shin-ing so bright, Si-lent and pure, won-drous light!
3. Glo-ry to God! Praise him on high! Sing ye "No-el!" Day is nigh!

Cold win-ter night, the frost ap-pears; Shep-herds keep watch by their fire.
What tid-ings brings it Is-ra-el? Can we new hope in it find?
All ye who dwell on earth be-low, Peace be to you, and good will.

Soft there a sound, far, far a-way; Is it the stream? Winds at play?
Good news it brings! "Fear not, I pray! Born is God's son, born to-day!
Come, let us go to Beth-le-hem; Fol-low the star, seek-ing him.

Nay, friend, it is the heav'n-ly choir, Ring-ing through-out the spheres.
God's gift of love to all man-kind, Our Lord, Im-man-u-el."
Let us a-dore and wor-ship still, In love and joy to grow.

From Japan to the World

Some hymns from Japan are becoming widely known and sung in other countries. Hymnals published by the Christian Council of Asia have helped music cross cultures. One of these traveling hymns is the Christmas carol, "Sheep Fast Asleep," which has begun to be sung by choirs and published in hymnals in North America. In Japan, Christmas is celebrated by many people beyond the Christian community as well as those within it, so Christmas music can help Christians interpret the meaning of this "imported" holiday.

MIWA Genzo (1871-1946) was born in Niigata (northern Japan). He graduated from Doshisha University and went on to teach at colleges in Kyoto. The translator is John Moss (UMC), now president of Keiwa Gakuin High School, Niigata.

TORII Chugoro (1898-1986) was born in Hokkaido, graduated from Meiji Gakuin and the Tokyo School of Music, and was a teacher of vocal music at Tokyo University of the Arts. He wrote the music for Miwa's Advent hymn, imitating the style of a French carol, with its simple beauty.

Prayers
Ishii Kin'ichi

Following a time of exhaustion and illness, ISHII Kin'ichi, a pastor, was led to write prayers and contribute them to the monthly church magazine, *Shinto no Tomo* ("The Companion of Faith"). His book, *For Days You Can't Pray*, brings together these prayers written between 1978 and 1984.[4]

The prayers, here translated by Kadota Noriko of Takarazuka, are arranged for use from early morning through the day.

The Only True God

Dear God,
    I was brought up knowing neither Christianity nor the church.
    In my house there were a Buddhist altar and a Shinto altar.
    As I was the eldest son, it was my duty to offer fresh water
        on the Shinto altar
    and the first cup of fresh-cooked rice on the Buddhist altar
        every morning.
    Every day I joined my hands in prayer to the Shinto gods and
        to Buddha.
    When I first went to church

I was surprised to find that there was no statue or anything
    to worship.
I wondered to what I should join my hands and pray.
As I study the Bible and continue church life
I am coming to understand vaguely that
there is the True God, which I cannot see or touch.
Now, no matter where I am,
whenever I close my eyes and join my hands in prayer
I can believe from the bottom of my heart
that there is the only True God Almighty,
the Creator of the world.

Freedom Through Faith

Dear God,
    I hate standing in a line.
    When I was a boy it was wartime.
    The power of the state made us stand in lines
    and put badges on in order to lead us into accepting one idea
        and one action.
    I was ignorant and obeyed the power.
    Since then I have been blaming myself for that and my
        heart hurts.
    Dear God,
    when I started to believe in you
    You forgave me and let me live with You as an individual
        person.
    You gave me freedom through faith.
    I thank you with all my heart.

Love That Can Feel Pain

Dear God,
    I was born here.
    I was brought up in that town.
    I studied in this school.
    I have been doing this job and that job.
    I can tell anybody, any strangers, where I live.
    I thought this was a common thing.
    When I met those who have been discriminated against,
    those who have received injury in the past,
    those who have handicaps of mind or body,
    and became their friend,
    I came to know that there are people who cannot tell their
        birthplace without feeling pain,
    people who become silent when it comes to what schools they
        went to,

people who cannot reveal their jobs, or addresses.
I have come to realize my ignorance,
How we torment those people by our casual words and deeds.
Let me love those who suffer from discrimination
and let me feel their pain.

Looking for a Light

Dear God,
One day I lost my way in the mountains.
I walked and walked but I could see only a few steps ahead
    of me.
Before long I saw a light in a house, and my heart was filled
    with joy at the thought that there was somebody living nearby
and that I was safe.
I felt a great hand leading me along the way.
I had been living in a deep, dark night,
and I thank God who gave me a Light as my guide.

PARK Heon Wook

Mr. Park, pastor of the Nishi Arai Korean Church in Tokyo, wrote
the following prayer especially for this book.

O Lord, our God,
We confess how inadequate we are to
Praise you.
You work in our lives, but the
Insecurity of life for us
As Koreans and minority peoples confuses us
And we are driven to despair,
Anger and distrust.
For us there seems to be no love or justice.

Yet in the darkness of the Cross,
We sense a darkness greater than our own.
In Resurrection we realize
You have prepared the light of love and justice.
And the power of this trust
Enables us to trust and
Praise you.

Constantly, Lord, we seek
Your Reviving Spirit for our lives
And for the life of the world.
We pray in the name of Jesus Christ. Amen.

Poems

HOSHINO Tomohiro (b. 1946)

On a June day in 1970, Hoshino Tomohiro was demonstrating gymnastics techniques for a club at the high school where he had begun teaching in April. A graduate of the School of Education, Gumma University, he had participated in gymnastics and mountain climbing since high school days. As he landed something went wrong, and he has been paralyzed from the neck down ever since.

During nine years spent in the hospital, he learned to write and draw, holding a brush in his mouth. He also heard the Bible read for the first time; in 1974 he was baptized. Five years later he returned to his home in Gumma Prefecture and was married in 1981.

Books, calendars, and postcards with Hoshino's poetry and paintings are well-known in Japan. *Ai, fukaki fuchi yori* (*Love from an Abyss*, 1981) and *Kaze no tabi* (*Journey of the Wind*, 1982) are bestsellers.[5]

Cherry Blossoms

Pushing my wheel-chair under a cherry tree
my friend pulled down a branch in full bloom
burying my face in its blossoms

With a surge of ungovernable joy
I bit off a mouthful of blossom
eating the pink-white petals
munching and munching

車椅子を押してもらって
桜並木の下まで行く
友人が枝を曲げると
私は満開の花の中に
埋ってしまった
湧き上ってくる感動を
おさえることができず
私は
口の周りに咲いていた
桜の花を
むしゃむしゃと
食べてしまった

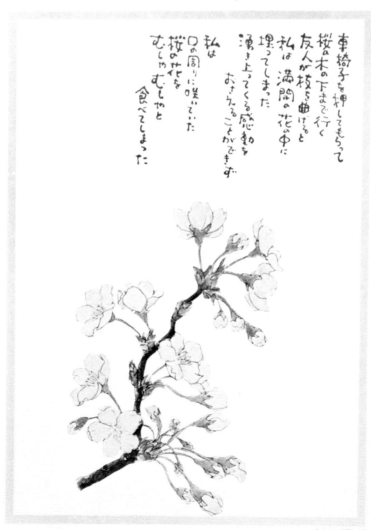

Meditation Through Words

Breaking Down a Wall in Japan

The Parable of the Hidden Treasure: Matthew 13:44

From a sermon delivered by TABUCHI Mayumi at Kobe Union Church, July 29, 1990.

The parable of the hidden treasure tells about a very big *joy* in heaven. This joy is so big that one can give up everything for it. When a man happens to find a treasure hidden in a field, how surprised he is! "He covers it up again, and is so happy that he goes and sells everything he has, and then goes back and buys that field." We can imagine how excited he is about his fortune. We don't know, however, whether it is morally good to buy a piece of land, secretly knowing it has a treasure in it.

But if we imagine that the person who discovers the treasure is one of the "sinners" in the Bible, like a tax collector or a prostitute who does not follow the sacred laws, then we may get a different idea about this parable, because the treasure is something that scribes or religious teachers cannot find.

The Gospels uncover Jesus' love toward the people who are discriminated against in society. Men and women who are called sinners listen to Jesus and receive the good news of God's forgiveness. And they come to feel confident in God's love.

In 1871 in Japan, *Kaiho Rei* (The Emancipation Edict) made the outcaste groups legal commoners for the first time. But the situation of discrimination against this group has continued for a long time and exists even now in modern Japan.

In the area of Mino, the present Gifu prefecture in central Japan, those from the discriminated-against buraku did not know the content of the Emancipation Edict, because the governing people had neglected to bring this good news (or, they might have thought, bad news) to the people in their region. But the rumor of this news reached the people at last. Yet they were not sure.

After a lot of discussion, the representatives of the discriminated-against group in Mino dressed up in their *kamishimo* (formal wear of that period) and went to the master's garden to ask about it. When at last the master appeared, the waiting men were astonished, because the master did not have his *mage* (topknot). As you know, samurai wore a topknot then. The master tried to ignore their stares and seemed to be ashamed of losing this sign of status. As the men examined his new hair style, they could accept the rumor as truth. Every one of them thought, "Doesn't his hair style make him just like one of us?"

The master in a feeble voice then told them about the new era. A man called Sakichi shouted out with joy, "Please tell us once more what you have said, sir." Again the master had to say that there were no longer any *eta* or *hinin*. [As many have pointed out, these are cruelly discriminatory terms. *Eta* literally means "full of filth," and *hinin*, "the non-people."]

What a memorable day it was for the people of the discriminated-against village of Mino! They were overjoyed, they shouted, and they even cried.

This story does not end here. In Mino, separating the "majority" group from the discriminated-against group was a "wall" of bamboo woods, about 23 meters, or 70 feet long. From the day the people heard the good news of the Emancipation Proclamation until the time all the trees were cut down, it took sixty years. The last negotiation with the landlord, in 1931, was the hardest. With an abrupt nod of his head, he finally gave permission for the "wall" to be removed, after 29 nights of persuasion by the patient, peace-loving people of the discriminated-against area.[6]

It is remarkable to witness the strength and tolerance of the people who were despised by society. When I heard the wonderful news that the wall of Berlin was broken down by the people, I remembered this story. Although there are many unseen walls among the people in Japan, this story inspires me with hope. The Kingdom of heaven may come like that!

So, friends, let's make constant, prayerful efforts based on our joyful faith in the Good News!

The Prodigal Son:
Living and Learning Together

OMIYA Hiroshi, pastor of Asagaya Church (Kyodan) in Tokyo, gave a series of Bible studies at an orientation for missionaries in 1989. Here are several sections of his presentation on Luke 15:11-32.

This story begins at the time the younger son asked his father to give him the portion of the father's property that would fall to him. According to Deuteronomy 21:17, the eldest son in the family was to get twice as much as the other brothers. Therefore, the younger son's portion was one-third. In the time of Jesus it was unusual for the father to distribute his property to his sons when he was still living. But the relation between parents and children tended to be influenced by arbitrariness and favoritism. In this case, the younger son forced his father in order in satisfy his own desire.

After a short time, he changed his property into money. Among the items of property, there were certainly the tokens of his family or furniture connected with reminiscences of his childhood. But he sold all of them. By this act, historical memory, which keeps each person's past as most precious, was erased, and there remained only money. This was the birth of an "economic animal." For him, love, trust and ethics seemed to be just a yoke to bind him. He went far away, where there was no restriction, and money was everything. . . .

The elder son thought of his own life in the father's house as life under a yoke, the same mentality as his younger brother's. That one went out, and this one stayed. But if one stayed home without having love for the father, it was the same as going out. He just lacked the courage to leave. Anyway, his heart "went away" from the father. In this sense, he was also a prodigal son. . . .

I'd like to consider this parable in the context of education. The father could not persuade the younger son to stay with him, and this made the elder son angry. Ephesians 6:1 tells us, "Fathers, do not provoke your children to anger." But this parable shows the reality of life. In Japan today there are many young people who cannot get married because they cannot get out of the "shelter" provided by their parents.

Prof. DOI Takeo, a noted psychiatrist, analyzed a mental feature peculiar to Japanese, and wrote *Amae no kozo* (*The Anatomy of Dependence*, 1973). *Amae* means "to be spoiled," in English, estimated as something negative. In Japanese, it is neither negative nor positive, but rather something tolerable, sometimes stimulating a parent's love. Through this *amae*, parents and children become mutually dependent, and it is rather difficult for children to be independent. The attitude of the father of the prodigal son seems to show *amae*, at least according to the elder son's opinion.

On the other hand, the elder son suffered from a lack of human sympathy. In Japan one journalist interviewed the students of a very famous university and was surprised by the fact that they did not show sympathy toward others. They entered that university through severe competition. For them, others were only the objects of competition, not neighbors. Thus, a competitive society produces "wealth without joy" through lack of sympathy. People demand that others become like themselves. This is the core of the problem of *ijime* (bullying): in school, students exclude those who are not like themselves and sometimes use violence toward them.

To live together, we must accept each other as we are. Does the parable of this prodigal son offer some suggestions for us?

Meditations Through Other Arts

Rudolf KUYTEN: Wood Carver

ABOUT THE CARVER: Rudy Kuyten, for many years a missionary in Japan from the Reformed Church in America, is pastor of the Church of the Twelve Apostles in Sapporo, Hokkaido. MIURA Ayako writes:

"Rudy Kuyten has experienced all the weaknesses and ugliness of human nature but has learned that Christ dealt with these things on the cross. So it is through his relationship with Jesus Christ that he has developed this warm and happy disposition."[7]

Christ-Head

I decided to read the gospels and every time I met Christ, I would sketch Him with my brush, like a *sumie* (brush painting). This became a wonderful study for me. I met Christ many times. Sometimes He was hungry, or wet from the rain, or tired, angry, lonely, strong, or sleepy.

With this rich experience I went to Lake Akan in Hokkaido to work for ten days among the Japanese and Ainu wood-carvers. There were five of us. During the day we worked in their shops and at night we had meetings, sharing our faith.

I worked for Mr. Nishiyama. One day he gave me a chisel with the words, "You carve Christ's head." So in 1969 in Akan I carved my first carving.

I carved this first head of Christ as an oriental, with a hair style like the young men of today. His beard is carved on only one side of His face, and His mouth is moving. He is speaking: "I am the Son of Man."

—Rudolf Kuyten (RCA)

KOSAKA Keiichi: Sculptor

Mr. Kosaka was born in 1918 in Aomori prefecture. He graduated from Tokyo University of Arts and won a prize as "New Artist of the Year" (1950). Among his sculptures are "Christ Bearing the Rupture of the World" (1970) at Osaka Expo, Christian Pavilion, and "The Woeful Mary" (1971) at Kyoto Notre Dame Gakuin. More recent works are "The Apostle John" for Aoyama Gakuin, Atsugi Campus, and "Nitobe Inazo" for the city of Towada (northern Japan).[8]

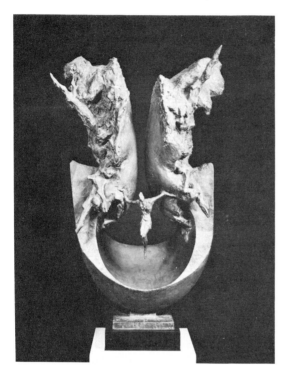

Christ Bearing the Rupture of the World.

"I shaped the body of the wounded Christ in the depth of the hollow of the split pomegranate.
The deep rent in the globe represents the sadness of human-kind—North and South Vietnams, North and South Koreas, East and West Germanies— human alienation."

WATANABE Sadao: Stencil Painter

Mr. Watanabe was born in Tokyo in 1913 and still lives there, near Takada-no-baba train station. As a boy, he was taken to church by a neighbor, and in 1930 was baptized, responding to Matthew 11:28.

Among other art techniques, he studied *katazome*, developed in Okinawa: "It is a unique craft of dying textiles through cut-out paper patterns." He utilizes this "to create unusual stencil paints on Japanese paper:

"After applying natural dyes on rice paper which are fixed with an ingredient from the astringent persimmon, he washes the paper.

"The Last Supper," 1970

Then, after putting rice paste upon the paper stencil, he applies the natural color all over, and washes the paper again."[9]

Exhibits of his work have been held in many countries of the world, sometimes garnering prizes. His work has often been reproduced in North America in magazines, books, and calendars.

SHIBATA Midori: Stencil Painter

SHIBATA Midori is an artist and musician, working with her husband at a "preaching point" in Otaru, Hokkaido. Ms. Shibata is active in organizing community concerts, teaches organ, and designs cards, offering envelopes, and covers for bulletins and programs. Reproduced here are an Easter card, on which the cross, birds, clouds and tomb suggest the kanji for the first part of "faith," *shin*, and a design of a growing plant that elaborates on the kanji for "love," *ai*.[10]

ENDO Kimiyoshi: Printmaker

Like my father, I, too, thought I would become a painter in my childhood. When I was a primary school boy, my mother gave me a collection of prints by Van Gogh. I spent most of my time painting, drawing and reading.

As a young man, I was struggling, something like Van Gogh. Death, the pain of life, sadness, suffering, anxieties, and love were unsolved problems for me. I could not love myself, or others, or God.

However, God showed love through the prayers of my family. Also Armin Kroehler, a missionary, encouraged me to live. Through him I had an opportunity to visit churches in the States. I made some woodblock prints on the themes of the Bible stories to give them as friendship presents.

During my study at seminary, I tried to complete a collection of "Jesus' Stories," but I could not finish. Since I have become a minister of a church, I have been too busy to do anything. But I make Christmas cards every year for the "Christmas Art Exhibition" sponsored by the Aizu Christian Church Coalition.

"I Am the Vine": This picture shows various scenes. 1) Jesus said, "I am the vine, and you are the branches" (John 15:5). We cannot do anything without him. 2) Jesus went up to the mountain and talked to his disciples, who gathered around him. Only Judas kept a good distance from him. Around this circle of disciples, people make a bigger circle, listening to Jesus talking. 3) Jesus said, "I came not to be served but to serve," and placed himself "under" every one of them. 4) The Lord was crucified on the hill of Golgotha. 5) You can imagine this any other way you wish.[11]

CHUJO Junko: Painter

Ms. Junko is an accomplished painter, pianist, and organist. Born in 1928, she attended Kwansei Gakuin University (KGU), Department of Christian Studies. She and her husband are members of Kwansei Gakuin Church. In her painting she especially enjoys using *iwaenogu*, colored rocks crushed finely.

In 1990 she received the Tessai Bijutsukan Prize for a painting in an exhibition sponsored by Takarazuka City and the Shorei Prize for a painting of the door of Lambuth Chapel at KGU. This painting, at left, is called "Inori no Ie," "The House of Prayer." She finds great meaning in Psalm 62 and Psalm 90:12.[12]

TANAKA Tadao: Painter

Mr. Tanaka's father was a Protestant minister. Tadao was born in Sapporo in 1903 and studied in Kyoto. He has received many prizes for his paintings and stained glass windows and is one of the preeminent Christian artists in Japan. He and his wife belong to Reinanzaka Church, Tokyo.[13]

Lithograph, "The Woman at the Well" (John 4:5-42)

Instructions for "Spirit of the Living God" Dance

This dance was created by KANEKO Machiko for a Japanese dance workshop at the Women's Conference, 1989 (see page 81). "Spirit of the Living God" was the theme song for the conference.

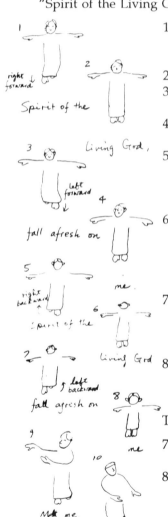

1. Extend arms at shoulder height, step forward (knees slightly bent) on right foot, sliding it along; slowly shift weight to that foot.
2. Slide left foot forward, even with the right.
3. Step back with right foot; then bring left foot back until it's even.
4. Step back with left foot, then slide right foot back until it's even, arms still extended.
5. Drop arms, step forward on right foot, lifting right arm, palm down, out to the right, about face high. Left arm is bent at elbow, palm up, going across body.
6. Step forward on left foot, bending knee a bit, bringing right arm down across body, palm up. Left arm goes straight out to the side, a little to the back, palm down. (Repeat 5 and 6.)
7. As you turn in a circle, starting on left foot, let right hand come back and, after a graceful wrist twist, put it up by forehead as if shading eyes. Left hand trails behind.
8. Stepping on right foot, with knee bent, lift left
   in prayer, turned a bit facing to the right.

THE SECOND TIME, REPEAT 1 TO 6.

7'. As in 1, slide right foot forward, arms extended.
8'. Bring left foot up past right foot, shifting weight to that foot, while bringing right foot up behind—almost as if to skip. Meantime, let hands go up toward left, moving them apart a little, as if flower petals are opening.[14]

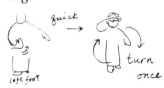

KITAMURA Soji: Calligrapher

When asked when he began studying calligraphy, KITAMURA Soji smiled and replied, "Since I was a child." Of course—every pupil practices writing with a brush, here in Japan, as a regular part of the school curriculum. In the last twenty years, however, he has developed a special interest and expertise in *sumie* (brush painting) and *shodo* (calligraphy), studying with a teacher based in Tokyo. Serving as minister of Eiko Church, Kobe—one of the largest Kyodan congregations in Japan—he also chairs the Kyodan Hymnal Committee.

Before beginning the following "lesson," he set out these materials: inkstone, inkstick (and a bottle of *sumi* ink), a small bottle with water, a piece of felt to be placed under the paper, paper weight, and brush. He began by passing on the instructions of his teacher, as to how best to prepare oneself spiritually to do calligraphy:

> Calligraphy is like the art of music: it's important to breathe quietly and have a calm heart. One should remember there is no chance to "redo" the writing, just as in music there is no repeating a passage to try to improve it, once it has been played.

"Here is a demonstration I've done in Texas and in Scotland. I begin by putting down a large piece of felt. Across the width I place a long piece of paper. While I'm doing this, I say, "You and I speak different languages: you speak English, and I speak Japanese. Jesus and others spoke Hebrew. Each of us also has a different way of writing. You write horizontally, left to right. (Then I write the word, 'PEOPLE,' at the left side of the paper.) The speakers of

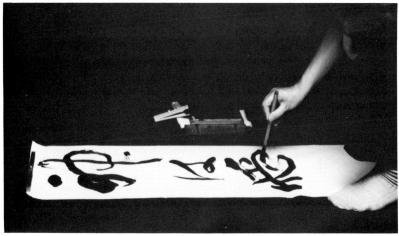

Calligrapher Kitamura at work

Hebrew write horizontally, right to left. (Beginning at the right side of the sheet, I write the four Hebrew consonants for "Yahweh.") I write from top to bottom. (Starting at the top of a sheet placed vertically across the other paper, I write the kanji for "God is love," *Kami wa ai nari*)

"Notice how the characters for 'love,' (*ai*) is right in the middle of the crossed paper [cross]. With all our differences, we are one in Christ, because God is love.[15]

TAKENAKA Masao:
Rice and Peace

The Chinese character for peace (*wa*) literally means harmony. It derives from two words: one is *rice* and the other is *mouth.** It means that unless we share rice together with all people, we will not have peace. When every mouth in the whole inhabited world is filled with daily food, then we can have peace on earth.

When we say that God is rice, we do not mean we should worship rice. We take rice as a symbol of God's gift of life. We stand by our radical monotheism. For us nature is a friend and companion. But we should resist the temptation to deify nature.

-—TAKENAKA Masao[16]

Takenaka's free-form "wa"

Origami

The dove is a sumbol of peace in many cultures. Many people now recognize the origami crane as a symbol of peace also (see the cover of this book). Design by Allison Young.

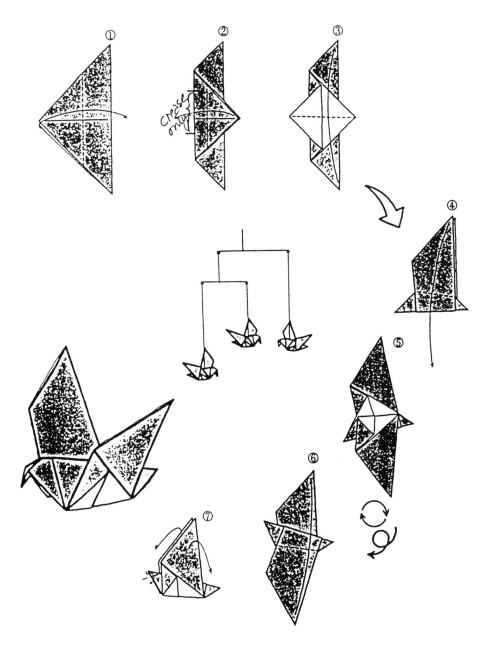

Ikebana

"Requiem"

A bamboo cross is arranged with a branch covered with hemlock and Old Man's Beard. the flowers are white Phalaenopsis (butterfly orchid); the stand is covered with moss.

Photo by Michael PRIEST

All the arrangements and descriptions are by Elaine JO (see note 14 in Part One.)

Moon-Viewing, In and Out of Season

The rabbit that the Japanese "see" on the full moon (page 10) is pounding rice. The moon-rabbit, borrowed from Chinese folklore, became a rice-pounder in Japan probably because the words for "full moon" and "rice pounding" sound the same (*mochitsuki*).

Traditionally, in mid-autumn a small, low table is set up in the eastern part of the room. On it are placed modest arrangements of seasonal flowers and grasses, such as *susuki* and pampas, and of rice balls and round fruits/vegetables, such as taro. It's all right to eat part of the arrangement, after you've enjoyed looking at it and the moon. If the full moon isn't visible, enjoy the round shape of a fan (*uchiwa*) or tray. Even if the moon can be seen, some people prefer to contemplate an artful representation on a scroll (*kakejiku*) or the moon's reflection in a small body of water.

Moonviewing arrangements are always very natural. The moon-viewing arrangement uses dried and bleached wild grass, loosestrife, and Chinese bell-flower. According to the Manyoshyu (an 8th century poetry collection) there were seven traditional flowering grasses of autumn: the bush clover, the pampas grass, the kuzu vine, the pink, the patrinia, the thoroughwort, and the balloon flower (bellflower)

Arrangement by Elaine Jo
Photo by Ogoshi Kenichi

Service of Meditation and Praise While Moonviewing

A service of worship related to moon-viewing would be especially appropriate in September or October.

Soloist: "Call to Wonder"

In Wonder

UEMATSU Isao
Trans. by J. M. N.

UEMATSU Isao

O - o - so - ra   ho - shi   to   tsu - ki   o
Great, o - pen sky,   stars of night and the moon,

na - ga - me - te   o   -   mo - u.
Look - ing   at them   all   in   won - der.

Call to Meditation

    Leader: Fair is the sunshine,
    ALL: Fairer still the moonlight,
    Leader & ALL: And all the twinkling starry host;
    Leader: Jesus shines brighter,
    ALL: Jesus shines purer
    Leader & ALL: Than all the angels heaven can boast.

[While someone plays or hums "Fairest Lord Jesus," spend time quietly looking at the moon—in the sky or in a moonviewing ikebana. Lead a guided meditation:]

    Think of the beauty of the full moon, now shining brightly,
      now partly hidden by thin clouds moving across its face.
    Recall the phases of the moon, as it seems to wax and wane.
    Now focus on the image of Jesus Christ, first, as a child,
      looking up into the vast night sky; then as an adult,
    searching for God's mysterious, marvelous ways; in the
        Garden of Gethsemane, probing both heavens and heart
        for God's will; as the resurrected expression of God's glory.

Hymn: "Fairest Lord Jesus," verses 1, 3

Leader: With each passage from the Psalms that refers to the moon, concentrate on a different part of the ikebana: stalk or stem, flower or grass, basket or flower holder. Keep the moon in view, as a symbol of God's constant care.

Psalm 8:1–4   Psalm 72:1–7, 12–14a, 18–19
Psalm 104:1–2, 5–9, 16–20, 24, 27–31a
(choose some verses)

Unison Prayer: O God of all creation, every creature, we praise you for the beauty that surrounds us, your power for good that frees us, the wonders in this world, and the breath that sustains us.

Help us recognize everything within us and among us that keeps us from reflecting your goodness. Infuse us with your shining grace. Move us to learn from nature, as from our neighbors, so that we may embrace your way with fresh resolve. Amen.

Leader: As I read some scenes from the ministry of Jesus, picture each one as a drama. Let your understanding and imagination select one detail or one insight from each scene. Try arranging these chosen elements in your mind, slowly, prayerfully. Perhaps you will "see" them as flowers or other natural elements of an arrangement. Perhaps they will together take another shape or sound as you reflect on the scriptural message.

Matthew 9:23-25   Mark 8:11-21   Luke 11:1-9
John 8:2-12   Luke 24:30-32
(choose 3)

A tape of traditional Japanese music could be played, such as music of *shakuhachi* (vertical flute) or *koto* (harp/zither.]

Leader: As you have created or re-created your arrangement, so Jesus of Nazareth worked at re-creating life. He healed children and adults, confronted self-righteous authorities, taught followers prayer as a strong strategy for living, forgave others, and joined in after-Easter eating with dull-eyed disciples who finally understood the unfolding of God's plan in Christ.

God is still re-creating life through the Spirit of Christ, through the church, through each person here. What do we need to do in our own lives to become more Christ-like, more compassionate, more creative? Let's consider these things, while we enjoy more of the nourishing gifts of God.

[Here have several people get up and quietly distribute napkins or *oshibori* (dampened washcloths, rolled up). They will then pass plates of simple food, such as seasonal fruits or vegetables, cheese and bread/crackers, rice balls and tea. Whenever possible, serve round, moon-shaped things. Or invite people to get up and help themselves, sparingly, from a buffet arrangement.

During the time of eating, play a tape of *"Kojo no tsuki"* (see page 8) or have someone play it on an instrument. It should be played several times, while people finish their small helpings.]

Hymn: "In Your Grace," verses 5, 6 (*"Kojo no tsuki"* melody on page 8; verses 1-4 on page 57.)

5. Seasons wheeling like the kite Whistling in the breeze;
   Spirit, give us in your time, Joy and work and ease.
   As we learn to watch the moon, Follow shadow, sun,
   We can learn to dance our love, See God's justice done.

6. Castle ruins still and firm, On the mossy stone;
   Walls enduring earthquake, fire, Overlooking town.
   God of saints and sinful ones, In your wide embrace,
   When the pebbles here are gone, Keep us in your grace.

Leader: Once more, let us think of the brilliance and loveliness of the moon—the way it leads us from season to season; the righteousness and peace that will exist even after the moon wears away; and above all these, the shining presence of Jesus Christ. Let us plan to let Christ's active example illumine us as we give and receive acts of kindness and justice.

Hymn: "All Creatures of Our God and King"

Benediction: Through the days to come, in every time of year or climate, may you know the luminous goodness of God, creator of all things, all people. Amen.

—Judy Newton

Benediction

For over thirty years in Japan an annual conference has been held in English for women. Usually about a hundred people assemble in late January. An increasing number of Japanese women are attending. This unique gathering goes on ecumenically year by year, with no central office.

These "parting words" are from the 1984 Women's Conference:

Go into the world
With a daring and tender love.
The world is waiting.
Go in peace.
And all that you do
Do it for love,
And by the Spirit of Jesus
Who is the Lord.

Part Four
Unfolding a Rainbow

J apan's Christians live beneath a Japan-shaped segment of God's overarching grace. The essays in Part Four represent only a few bands from that piece of colorful prism, some short reports from the life of the church. From people in this book you have heard deep concerns about themes worth your further unfolding: values in a secularized society, the environment, peoples excluded from a society prizing homogeneity, world peace in light of national experiences of war, mission with neighbors beyond Japan's shores. Our hope is that you will continue to discover ways to understand and share these questions and visions where you are.

> "I pray that this book may be used to God's honor and glory."
>
> —TAKAHASHI Kiku (introduced on page 44)

Church and Other Music

In Japan today the stately *Noh* drama of the fourteeenth century is still performed, as is the 300-year-old *kabuki*, or *bunraku* (puppet) theater. Theater-goers can also see performances of experimental drama and Shakespeare. In the same way, one can hear music in a great variety of styles, even in church. Several Christians describe how music influences them and their community of faith.

Invited by Music

During the last part of the Pacific War—I should say the Fifteen-Year War (1930-1945)—I encountered Christianity when I was evacuated to a small village, called Yamazaki-cho, in southwestern Hyogo Prefecture. My sister was teaching music at a primary school in a small town nearby. At that time, we could rarely listen to music. People even hesitated to practice the piano.

One evening, my sister and I were walking homeward. Suddenly the sound of an organ swelled. We hadn't noticed there was a small church halfway down the hill. Quietly we went into the church, drawn by the music.

It may have been a Sunday evening service. Anyway, I remember the pastor approaching us at the end of the service, welcoming us with a smile. I felt someone had mysteriously guided us there, because both my sister and I, without consulting each other, had gone straight into the church. . . .

My elder sister and I were baptized on the fifth of September, 1948, and my mother and younger sister were baptized the same year on Christmas Day.

—TAKEMURA Yasuko[1]
(introduced on page 32)

Affirming God's Gifts Within Japanese Culture

From 1958 to 1961, George Gish, Jr., served as a short-term missionary in Nagoya, then returned to the U.S. for studies on Japan and ethno-musicology at the University of Michigan. In 1968 he returned to Japan as a United Methodist missionary to work with churches in communications, education and local church evangelism. As a musician, he has learned the ancient art of the *biwa*, the traditional Japanese lute. Gish studied the Satsuma *biwa* from the late TSUJI Seigo, and the medieval Heike *biwa* from the late TATEYAMA Kogo. His activities to promote *biwa* music have helped keep these forms from becoming extinct.

"One question I am often asked by church friends is, 'What does your interest in the *biwa* have to do with being a missionary?'

"In reality, the world of Japanese traditional music is world apart from the average modern-day Japanese people, including those in the church. This results in an identity crisis for most Japanese,

who have been cut off from their own cultural roots during the past century of state-controlled modernization.

"While it is true that Western forms seem to dominate the outward cultural expressions today, at the same time many underlying attitudes remain unchanged. By learning a traditional performing art form, I have been able to bridge partially the chasm between Japanese church musicians and others in the church, who have been alienated from their own traditional culture.

"Wherever the church is found, it is challenged to express the gospel in new and meaningful ways, making creative use of the variety of gifts found in each culture. For me, helping to keep alive a tradition over a thousand years old has been one small way of affirming God's gifts within Japanese culture, as well as opening up the potential of new forms of expression for Christian worship that are rooted in Japan's cultural soil.

—George Gish

Rock Concerts in Wakamatsu-Sakaemachi Church

As assistant pastor, KATAOKA Etsuya has been involved in a project of "Junior Church" for teenagers at the Wakamatsu-Sakaemachi Church (Kyodan; Fukushima Prefecture). Many church buildings in Japan are modern in architecture and construction, but this Junior Church was held in an older, traditional style building called "Gospel House" near the church. The program included a short service for junior and senior high school students and help in studying such subjects as English and mathematics. Kataoka spent a lot of time with the young people. Some had "dropped out" of school under the tremendous tension of the competitive entrance examination system. They liked to come to Junior Church where nobody judged their "punk" fashions.

One day Kataoka suggested that they have a musical band. He himself was a lover of guitar music. Immediately some were eager to join up, and eventually they started to practice in the Gospel House. One of the students recalls, "It didn't necessarily have to be music. It didn't matter what we did then. But we got turned on by the musical instruments."

A breakthrough came for them when the church invited "The Messengers," a popular professional band, to give a concert. The church band performed in that concert, too. Then, even more exciting, The Messengers gave the small band a three-hour lesson after the concert.

From that time on, the church became "famous" among the young people in that region. Kataoka asked them to make one promise: to see one another once a week in the Sunday morning service for junior and senior high school students. Around thirty or forty young people agreed. During the thirty-minute Sunday service, Kataoka played guitar, gave a short message, and offered prayers.

Now the program is growing, and the church has two concerts for the bands every year. Each concert draws about two hundred young people and their families. Their colorful hair styles and fashions can be easily imagined. The tough sounds of electric guitars and drums are like a thunderstorm. The members of Wakamatsu-Sakaemachi Church support this young assistant pastor and hope that they can someday build a new, larger hall nearby.[2]

Church Life

Japanese Holidays and the Church Calendar

We celebrated the beginning of the new year by attending the service of Holy Communion at Ginza Church (Tokyo). This service is one example of how churches have adapted Japanese traditions.

A visit to a Shinto shrine at the beginning of the year is one of the most widespread traditions in Japan. During the first three days of January nearly three-quarters of the population make such visits; probably most make this annual pilgrimage more because it is the thing to do than from deep religious conviction.

Churches in Japan sometimes attempt to incorporate traditional practices and give them richer meaning. Many churches hold New Year's Day services, often uniting on a sub-district level. In our East Tokyo sub-district, the union service also includes the ordination of new clergy. (Districts and sub-districts are regional units of the Kyodan.)

This "indigenization of the gospel" has reached to other celebrations as well.

At many churches the first Sunday following Coming of Age Day (January 15) is used to recognize those who have turned 20 during the past year. The Kyodan has designated February 11, a national day commemorating the first emperor's founding of the nation, as the "Day to Protect Freedom of Religion" and holds rallies and peaceful demonstrations.

The spring and fall equinoxes are closely associated with Buddhist funerary customs and the veneration of the dead. These days are for visiting family graves, washing the stones, then setting up flowers, burning incense, and offering prayers. Some churches that have common grave sites for their members hold ceremonies at the graves on the equinoxes. Others visit the common grave on Easter Sunday afternoon to hold a service and deposit the ashes of members who have died during the year.

The most widespread incorporation of Japanese tradition for children into the church is a service of blessing held in mid-November. This is related to Shichi-Go-San (means "seven-five-three"), a festival held in Shinto shrines on November 15 (not a holiday). Boys aged three and five and girls aged three and seven are dressed up and taken to the shrines for special services. In the Christianized version, families bring their three-, five- and seven-year-olds to the church for a service of blessing, often held on the Sunday nearest November 15.

—from a letter by John W. Krummel (UMC)

Women and the Church

Women's roles in Japanese society are shifting and enlarging. For example, on May 17, 1985, the Diet, or parliament, passed the Equal Opportunity in Employment Law. This law reflects and supports the gains Japanese women have made in employment. But at the same time because legislation to protect women's health and safety at work was lost and the new law depends on voluntary implementation, much of the stuffing was removed from the new law.

"A woman holding a broom"—that is the literal meaning of *fujin*, one kanji for "woman". For that reason, in 1988 DOI Takako persuaded her political party to change the name of its Women's Section from *fujin* to *josei*, (womanhood, corresponding to *dansei*, manhood).

In the church, the group for married women is *fujinkai* (women's association). What actually is expected of women in the church? What roles do they take?

Marjorie A. Powles reported on "Japanese Women and the Church," for the World Mission Sub-Committee of the Anglican Church of Canada. Her report drew this comparison:

> In traditional Japanese drama—Kabuki and Noh—there are black-robed and hooded figures who change scenery and costumes in plain view of the audience, fitting like shadows behind the actors. In Bunraku, the puppet drama, these "shadows" actually manipulate the life-sized puppets. The audience sees them but does not see them. To me, this describes women in the church. They keep the drama working, sometimes even to manipulate it, but they are largely unseen and receive no credits for the performance.[3]

YAMASHITA Akiko, writing in an NCCJ publication, listed ways the women's society is referred to, even by the women themselves: "a humble and invisible voluntary workforce; mothers of the church; acting 'wives' of the pastor." She sees the church as separated into "men's/official" church and "women's/supportive" church, with little communication between these churches.

Though much about women and the church has negative overtones, let me affirm that women in the church are studious, dedicated, and energetic. While somewhat fearful or guilty at not being home, women express feelings of liberation at having new experiences in the wider world. In fact there is great concern among the church women for the oppressed, including Koreans and migrant workers from other Asian countries. Many women work in interchurch activities, such as the World Day of Prayer.

Ms. Powles is convinced that:

We in the West have much to learn from Christian women in Japan who are venturing into new relationships and types of service, using skills learned over generations of serving with grace, while maintaining a sense of identity and strength.

—Tabuchi Mayumi

Celebrating Faith and Culture:
Dancing in the Church

At times when faith and culture mix, the result can be a dramatically different way of praising God. Recently our Korean congregation in Kawasaki (between Yokohama and Tokyo) honored three women as *kwonsa*, a position of honor usually accorded older women in the church.

As a part of the celebratory party that followed worship, three teenage young women and their teacher gave a program of Korean drumming. Such performing on small drums, usually played while seated, is an important part of Korean culture. As the drumming continued, the teacher began to dance about the room in a Korean style that expressed the feelings of the joyful day.

Then, quite spontaneously, the oldest of the new *kwonsa* rose from her chair and joined in the dancing. Her movement encouraged others and one by one the other honored women joined her.

More and more women joined the dancing. Then some men began to dance. Now the rest of the congregation began to clap their hands with the rhythm of the drumming and dancing, until every single person was involved.

The spirit of celebration begun in worship had continued, as members of an oppressed minority shared from the depths of their spirituality and cultural pride. And in both worship and dancing God was praised.

—Philip Park[4]

The Church Reaches Out

TAKATSU Ryohei (b. 1953)

Former Missionary in Nepal, Company Employee
Sendai

1. What elements of culture in Japan would you most like to share with people in North America?
That we introduce such and such items of Japanese culture to

 people in North America is not so important, in my opinion. It is important to encounter individuals through various personal contacts. Therefore, we should start from the point of learning each other's languages. Only this effort to communicate can be the basis of a sound relationship.

We must realize that it is the work of the Spirit that makes it possible for us to communicate. So we are living with the Spirit, between the story of Babel (Genesis 11) and Pentecost (Acts 2).

2. What are your hopes and aims for the 1990s?

I would like to improve communication levels all around me. In our society, so often language seems not to "work." First of all, I want to be able to talk more meaningfully with my wife. Then I can widen this effort in the company where I work and in the church which our family attends.

3. What passage in the Bible do you find most striking?

The story of the blind man in John 9, especially in verse 3.

Notes and Permissions

Preface

Some Church-related terms and abbreviations used in this book are:

Gakuin	(private) school; jogakuin/jogakko—women's school
JNAC	Japan-North America Committee on Cooperative Mission
KCCJ	Korean Christian Church in Japan
Kyodan	Nihon Kirisuto Kyodan: United Church of Christ in Japan
NCCJ	National Christian Council in Japan
PCUSA	Presbyterian Church (U.S.A.)
RCA	Reformed Church in America
UCBWM	United Church of Christ Board for World Ministries
UCC-DWO	United Church of Canada, Division of World Outreach
UMC	General Board of Global Ministries, United Methodist Church

Part One: Sampling the Culture

1. Kanji development chart prepared by Masako RYAN (UCC-DWO).
2. A former short-term missionary (UMC) and long-time resident of Japan, now living in Claremont, Calif.
3. Stories retold by Judy Newton.
4. Adapted from version by Margery L. Mayer, in *With Pen and Brush* Friendship Press, 1957).
5. Poem first appeared in *Shishu: Nihom no kora (Collection of Poems by Japanese Children.* Tokyo: Nihon Hyojun, 1988. Translation by HIRAMATSU Kimiyo; cicada illustration by her son, Tomoru James, age 14.
6. From *Mainichi Daily News,* June 8, 1990. Used by permission of Marist Brothers International School.
7. H. Neill McFarland. From *Daruma: The Founder of Zen in Japanese Art and Popular Culture* (Tokyo and New York: Kodansha, 1987). Used by permission of the publisher.
8. From *An Invitation to Kokeshi Dolls* (Hirosaki: Tsugaru Shobo, 1982), with permission of Ms. Stevens.
9. Most of the proverbs are included in *Intermediate Japanese Reader* (Tokyo: Institute of Japanese Studies, 1986) of the Franciscan language school.

    ANSWERS TO PROVERB PUZZLE:
    l-j, 2-h, 3-d, 4-g, 5-i, 6-e, 7-b, 8-a, 9-f , l0-c.

10. Translated by NISHIZAKI Kazuko from preface by ASAI Toru to *Ainu no Yukara: Kamigani to ningen no monogatari (Yukara: The Ainu Epic: The Story of the Gods and People.* Tokyo: Chikuma Shobo, 1987).
11. CHIKAP Mieko, from "I Am Ainu, Am I Not?" in *AMPO: Japan Asia Quarterly Review* (Vol. 18, Nos. 2-3, 1986). Used by permission of *AMPO.*
12. From *Bingata* (Okinawa: Marumasa, 1989). Photo: Rodney O. Absher.
13. Ms. Yamamoto was born into "an ordinary non-Christian family. My encounter with Christianity was through the Christian schools," she said. According to her questionnaire reply "Christians here and abroad should value their different tasks and hopes in mission and help each other, as they can." She is active in the Theological Association of Women Ministers.

14. Elaine Jo of the PCUSA is a Master Teacher of the Ichiyo School of Ike-bana. For information about English books and correspondence courses, write The Ichiyo School of Ikebana, Ichiyo Kaikan, 4-17-5 Nakano, Nakano-ku, Tokyo 164, Japan.
15. Barbara Mensendiek (UCBWM) is a friend of Mrs. Maehara through the Women's Fellowship of Hirose Kahan Church, Sendai. Photo: Barbara.
16. Published by Women's Society, Tokyo Union Church, 1978.
17. Translated by Tabuchi Mayumi from articles by Mrs. Kobayashi in *Shinto no tomo (The Companion of Faith)*, Oct. 1988, Jan. 1990.
18. Translated by Judy Newton from Kobayashi Katsuko, *Oishii mono o tsukuro (Let's Make Delicious Things.* Tokyo: Fuzanbo, 1988). Illustrated by KAMIHO Takiko, a Christian artist who lives near Tokyo. Used by permission of the author and the artist.

Part Two: Meeting the People

1. Quote and information about Ms. Takemura from an interview by Dave Swain (UMC) in the *Kyodan Newsletter*, Mar. 30, 1990. Translation of questionnaires are by William Elder (UMC), Robert Stieber (UCBWM), Margaret Warren (UMC), authors and friends.
2. In the *International Review of Mission*, Oct. 1986.
3. Hymn included in *The Way of Faithfulness* (see inside back cover).
4. In *Japan Christian Quarterly*, Summer, Fall 1989, Spring 1990.
5. Jim Joyce is a UMC missionary.
6. Mr. Arimura's cartoon is from Volume 3 of the Kamayan series. Used by permission of artist and Japan Democratic Press Publishing Center.
7. From *JOCS Bulletin*, May 1972.
8. Newspaper article quoted on pages 50-51 is from *Kahoku Shimpo*, Sendai, Jan. 19, 1990. Translation by Martha Mensendiek, Kyoto (UCBWM) approved by Mr. Motoshima. Two following paragraphs based on reports in *Mainichi Daily News* and *Japan Times.*.
9. From *Nagasaki Shicho e no 7300 tsu no Tegami (7300 Letters to the Mayor of Nagasaki)*, ed. by HARADA Naoo (Tokyo: Komichi Shobo, 1989). Translated by Mayumi.
10. Adapted from report in Japan YWCA's English newsletter, Nov. 1989.

Part Three: Folding in Prayer

1. Compiled from various sources, including an interview with a nephew of Nishimura, by Sue Althouse (PCUSA). Some material for commentary on the two hymns is from *Sambika Ryakkai: Kashi no bu* (1954) and *Kyoku no bu* (1955) issued by the Kyodan Board of Publications (brief background of hymns in the *Sambika, Hymnal*). Permission to use music from *Sambika*, (Kyodan, 1976), for these two hymns and words to "Jesus Loves Me" granted by Hymnal Committee of the Kyodan Board of Publications.
2. From an article by Margaret L. Olson (Lutheran Church) in *Japan Christian Quarterly*, Fall 1975.
3. Words and those on page 81 copyright 1990 by Judith May Newton.
4. From "Afterword" of *Inorenai hi no tame ni (For Days When You Can't Pray.* Tokyo: Kyodan Board of Publications, 1985). Prayers (translated by Kadota Noriko) printed with publisher's permission.

5. Pages 62, 63. Art and poetry from Hoshino Tomohiro, *Kaze no tabi (Journey of the Wind.* Tokyo: Rippu Shobo, 1982). English translation by Kyoko and Gavin BANTOCK (Tokyo: Rippu, 1988). Photo of page by FUKAI Jun. Permission to reproduce page granted by Mr. Hoshino.
6. Translated and adapted by Mayumi from "A Distant Roar of Thunder," in TANAKA Tatsuo, *Hisabetsu Buraku no Minwa (Stories of the Discriminated-Against Buraku),* Vol. 2 (Tokyo: Akashi Shoten, 1986). Used by author's permission.
7. MIURA Ayako, a well-known Christian novelist and essayist, in Preface to Rudy Kuyten, *Koko (Wood Carving.* Tokyo: Billy Graham, 1978). Mr. Kuyten's quote and carving from his book also; used with his permission. Photo by Fukai Jun.
8. Photo supplied by Mr. Kosaka. Quoted description in *Kosaka Keiji: Sakuhinshu (Works of Kosaka Keiji.* Tokyo: Kyubi Kikaku, 1984).
9. From Takenaka Masao, *Watanabe Sadao: Seisho Hangashu (Biblical Prints by Sadao Watanabe.* Tokyo: Shinyoko, 1986). Translated by Judy from introduction. Photo of Last Supper print by Shoji Hiroshi. Used by permission of Mr. Watanabe.
10. Prints used by permission of artist.
11. Print used by permission of artist.
12. Photo of print supplied by the artist.
13. Photo of lithograph used by permission of Mr. Tanaka.
14. Mrs. Kaneko has been trained in the Hanayagi School of Japanese Dance. She has combined traditional dance movements with her Christian witness; she is a member of Kobe Union Church. Photos by SHIMIZU Shigeru. Chart by Mayumi. Authorized adaptation of "Spirit of the Living God" by Word of God, Ann Arbor, Mich. Copyright 1935, 1963. Moody Bible Institute of Chicago. Used by permission.
15. Photos of Kitamura and calligraphy by Fukai Jun.
16. From Takenaka Masao, *God Is Rice: Asian Culture and Christian Faith,* Geneva: World Council of Churches, 1986), by permission of WCC. Calligraphy created and supplied by Mr. Takenaka.
17. Mr. Uematsu is an Anglican liturgist living near Tokyo. Translation by Judy Newton and Barbara Mensendiek.

Part Four: Unfolding a Rainbow

1. From Takemura Yasuko, *Onna yo, gen o narase (Women, Play Your Harps.* Tokyo: Toyo Shobo, 1985. Translated by Mayumi.
2. Translated by Mayumi from *Shinto no tomo (The Companion of Faith),* Kyodan magazine, Oct. 1989. Used by permission of publisher.
3. From Marjorie Powles, "Japanese Women and the Church," *Japan Christian Quarterly,* Winter 1987. Ms. Yamashita's article, summarized here, is "Nihon to Kirisuto kyokai ni okeru bosei genri ("Principle of Motherhood in the Japanese Church"), in *Deai: Kirisuto kyo to Sho Shukyo (Encounter: Christianity and Other Faiths.* Kyoto: NCCJ Center for the Study of Japanese Religions, Dec. 1989).
4. Philip Park is a PCUSA missionary.
5. Permission to reprint "Sayonara, Goodbye" from *Kodomo Sambika* granted by Hymnal Committee of Kyodan Board of Publications.